NORTH
CASCADES
HIGHWAY

NORTH CASCADES HIGHWAY

Washington's Popular and Scenic Pass

JoAnn Roe

Montevista Press
Bellingham, Washington

Published by
Montevista Press
Bellingham, Washington 98226

Manufactured in the United States of America

Cover art by Frederick L. Hubbard
Cover photos courtesy of Shafer Museum, Winthrop, Washington

The excerpt on pp. 58-59 is from *My Story* by Mary Roberts Rinehart,
copyright 1931. Reprinted by permission of Henry Holt & Co., Inc.

Contents

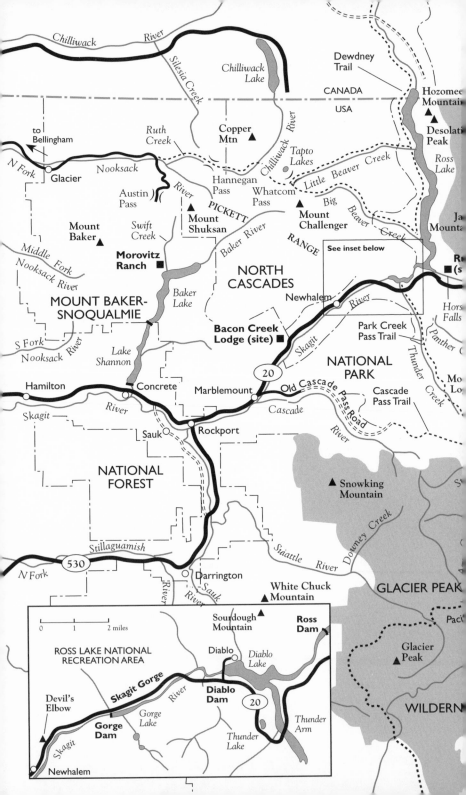

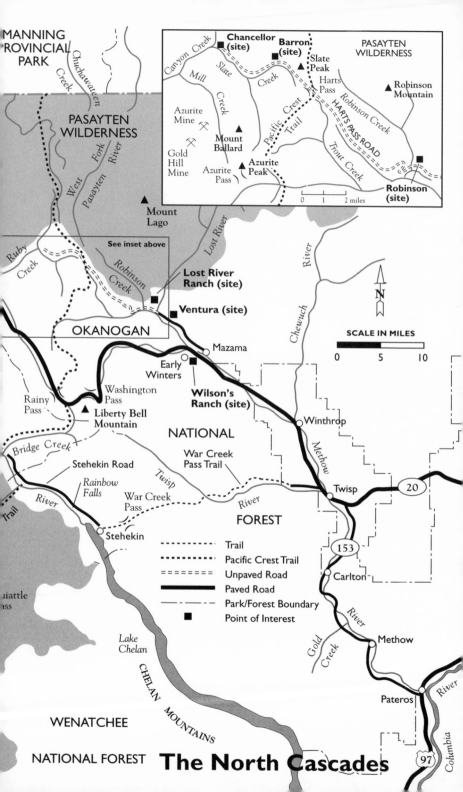

MANNING
ROVINCIAL
PARK

Chuchawateen Creek

PASAYTEN
WILDERNESS

West Fork Pasayten River

Ruby Creek

Robinson Creek

Mount Lago

OKANOGAN

Lost River Ranch (site)

Ventura (site)

Lost River

Mazama

Early Winters

Wilson's Ranch (site)

Rainy Pass

Washington Pass

Liberty Bell Mountain

NATIONAL

Bridge Creek

Stehekin Road

Rainbow Falls

War Creek Pass Trail

Twisp River

War Creek Pass

Stehekin

FOREST

Trail

iattle ass

Lake Chelan

CHELAN MOUNTAINS

WENATCHEE

NATIONAL FOREST

Chewuch River

Winthrop

Methow

Twisp

20

153

Carlton

Gold Creek River

Methow

Pateros

River

Columbia

97

The North Cascades

SCALE IN MILES

0   5   10

N

Trail
Pacific Crest Trail
Unpaved Road
Paved Road
Park/Forest Boundary
Point of Interest

Inset

Canyon Creek

Mill Creek

Slate Creek

Chancellor (site)

Barron (site)

Slate Peak

Harts Pass

PASAYTEN WILDERNESS

Robinson Creek

Robinson Mountain

Azurite Mine

Mount Ballard

Gold Hill Mine

Azurite Pass

Azurite Peak

Pacific Crest Trail

HARTS PASS ROAD

Trout Creek

Robinson (site)

See inset above

0   1   2 miles

Preface

The North Cascades Highway winds along a wild and scenic river, passes three lakes, affords panoramas of perpetually snow-covered peaks, and reaches a summit of 5,477 feet at Washington Pass before a steep descent into the Methow Valley. Like turning a page, a traveler goes from the western side's seacoast and urban ambience with towering firs and cedars to the eastern side's semi-arid wilderness, punctuated by dramatic post-glacial crags fragrant with the scent of pine, flattening into rolling ranch country.

One of America's newest scenic highways, the North Cascades Highway was completed twenty-five years ago and dedicated on September 2, 1972. Unlike earlier roads, it incorporates aesthetics as well as practicality. Judicious cutting of trees enables travelers to see the vistas and roadside enhancements of grass and flowers. The passage opens to a public of varying physical capabilities the possibility of exploring the inner vastness of the range, previously accessible only to the most physically fit through long, arduous hikes or horseback treks. As a scenic highway, the road belongs to every citizen. It is my hope that all travelers will respect its beauty by keeping it clear of roadside trash and damage.

A thirty-year resident of the state of Washington, I have wandered the valleys and high country of the North Cascades on foot and on horseback. The stillness on those high trails makes me feel like whispering. The vistas expand my spirit and inspire meditation about life. Noisy, rushing streams speak of Nature's busy, ongoing resculpting of the range, transporting eroding materials to carve new valleys and cliffs, all the while nourishing the forests and greenery with life-giving water. Humans have a place in these mountains, along with deer, bear, and cougar, as long as they respect the life that was there before two-footed creatures joined the four-footed. The North Cascades Mountains are Washington's treasure, not for the gold they once reluctantly gave up, but for the role the range plays in regulating the climate and fertility of the entire state.

1. GEOLOGY OF THE NORTH CASCADES

Close your eyes and transport yourself back in time a billion years. North America was low-lying and the oceans inundated the land at least three times. The Cascade Range was merely a trench. The terrain was barren, a moonscape strewn haphazardly with silt and rock. Gradually the silt and rock fragments washed into the trench, filling it. A massive earthquake ensued, extruding rock and sediment from the trench, sending them upward to form mountains far higher than those of today.

Eons passed. Storms raged across the ragged earth. The ancient North Cascades were battered and eroded. The oceans returned to drown the peaks once again.

Submarine volcanoes roared to the surface, sending molten rock far above the oceans to cool and reconstitute the North Cascades. A tropical climate encouraged the development of primitive creatures. Volcanic pressures again built up along both sides of the Cascades. In a pincers movement the mountains were forced upward and outward. Materials crystallized by pressure and heat formed gneiss, a banded or striped granite commonly seen between Newhalem and Granite Creek.

The North Cascades "Island"

About fifty million years ago an ancient sub-continent attached itself to North America somewhere west of the Okanogan Valley. The force of the joining fractured the edges, leaving such prominent faults as the

Straight Creek (lying almost due north/south through Marblemount to Stevens Pass), the Entiat (which angles northwesterly from Wenatchee), the Gardner Mountain (parallel to and south of the Methow Valley), and the Pasayten (parallel to the other two from south of Okanogan). A different remnant of the cataclysmic joining is evident in the movement of big chunks of land between the faults, called *graben*. The Chiwaukum graben extends from south of Leavenworth northerly to a point south of Marblemount. The Methow graben lies south of the highway between Twisp and Early Winters. Rocks in the latter include considerable numbers of sea shell fossils, evidence of a sedimentary birthplace.

Thirty to eighty million years ago, a time when prehistoric animals walked the earth, another upheaval propelled the very footings of the mountains far from the site of the eruptions. Greenstone flowed over layers of earlier material to form the summit of Jack Mountain and parts of Mount Shuksan. Molten granite oozed upward, extending from Redoubt Mountain in Canada across Mount Challenger in the Pickett Range, and from Mount Triumph to a point west of Newhalem.

Farther east a different type of molten mass formed the golden-orange rocks that constitute Liberty Bell Mountain in Washington Pass, Golden Horn Peak, Mount Silverstar, and other peaks adjacent to today's North Cascades Highway. Along Early Winters Creek a similar substance baked earlier shales into an almost ceramic substance.

Sandstone sloughed off the shoulders of the eastern slopes of the North Cascades to form the layered cliffs above Mazama and the Chuckanut Mountains near Bellingham. Fossils near Bellingham give evidence of jungle-like climate and foliage.

Massive slippages tilted the mountain peaks and foothills and, at one time, a rippling earthquake gently folded the entire range like ribbon candy. During another earthquake the ancient Skagit River, coursing lazily along through a relatively level bed, was raised high into the mountains. Skagit Gorge, formed by the river on its way back to the sea, once was a formidable barrier for travelers, lying between today's Ross Dam and Newhalem.

On the east the Methow River chewed its way toward the Columbia from Rainy Pass to Pateros. En route its flow was amplified by vigorous streams such as Brush, Rattlesnake, and Robinson Creeks, and the Lost and Chewuch Rivers.

The Ice Age

About a million years ago, the streams of the North Cascades were overwhelmed by the continental glacier that poured relentlessly southward from Canada. A portion of the glacier sought an easy path across the valley between the Olympic and Cascades Mountains, covering today's Whatcom County with ice as much as a mile thick and petering out a bit south of Seattle, leaving a terminal moraine (a mound of sand, rock, and silt). Icy fingers pushed rocks and debris up the Skagit River Valley to Newhalem, damming up the Baker River Valley around Lake Shannon.

On the east side another finger of ice rolled over the Methow Valley and scoured out Lake Chelan, fifty miles long and more than four hundred feet deep, a freshwater fjord. Glacial action is vividly evident in the sheer precipices of Goat Wall in the upper Methow Valley.

Melt fed into the basin between the Olympics and Cascades to admit the ocean through the Strait of Juan de Fuca, forming Puget Sound as we know it today.

East of the Cascades a glacier lay stubbornly in place across the ancient Columbia River bed around Bridgeport, while melting waters built up behind an ice barrier farther east that geologists call "Lake Missoula." When sufficient pressure fractured the barrier, a torrent of water descended west and south to slam against the Bridgeport glacier and be deflected south, reaming out the Grand Coulee, milling around in a vast lake near the Tri-Cities, and eventually crashing through Columbia Gorge on a path to the sea. This cataclysm may have been repeated several times.

Near the end of the Ice Age Mount Baker erupted, forming a basalt cinder cone at its base; lava flowed for twelve miles down Sulphur Creek.

The "Little Ice Age"

During a routine field trip to the North Cascades foothills in 1995, Western Washington University student Dori Kovanen noticed a hill along Mosquito Lake Road (about halfway between Bellingham and Mount Baker) that appeared to be a moraine. Kovanen found that the rocks within were not from Canada (the last ice age) but were a distinctive mix of red and black lava from Mount Baker and yellowish dunite with green crystals found only on the Twin Sisters formation. Kovanen discovered other such moraines on the north and south forks of the Nooksack River. With the assistance of Professor Don Easterbrook, she took core samples at key points. The findings seem to indicate that a "Little Ice Age" occurred about 2,000 years later than previously thought. Substantiating the theory, National Park Service archaeologist Robert Mierendorf maintains that the "Little Ice Age" lasted from about A.D. 1300 to 1850. Much colder temperatures than usual were recorded in the North Cascades during the gold rush of the 1800s and early 1900s. World temperatures also verify a colder trend during those centuries.

Recent North Cascades Activity

In 1843, Mount Baker erupted to throw ashes as far as the Skagit Valley. Significant steam eruptions occurred in 1854, 1858, 1870, and 1975.

In 1900 an earthquake on the south fork of the Nooksack River caused changes that raised the riverbed in one location seventy feet above its former level. In the riverbed long seams opened through which gravel was forced upward into ridges ten to twenty feet high.

Evidence of this turbulent history is written on the mountains, if one knows where to look. "Post piles" (columnar basalt) are seen along the Mount Baker access road. To the east of Mount Baker and visible from the North Cascades Highway near Newhalem, the Pickett Range is carved from Skagit gneiss and fringed by the white scallops of glacial cirques, as is Mount Shuksan. Peaks above the upper Methow River are chiseled from Golden Horn batholith. The ridges of the Chuckanut Mountains trace the ancient folding of sandstone and shale. Basalt outcroppings occur many places in the Cascades. The Twin Sisters, looming above the Skagit Valley, is a formation composed entirely of dunite, a material containing the mineral olivine. Dunite comes from the earth's mantle with such a high melting point that it has retained its identity through continental crust eruptions.

Such, then, is the geological setting for the search for a practical mountain crossing through the North Cascades, a goal finally reached in 1972 when the North Cascades Highway was opened. Until then no road existed across the mountains for over 100 miles, from the Hope–Princeton Highway at the north to Stevens Pass at the south.

2. THE NATIVE AMERICANS

Virtually nothing was known about post-glacial Native Americans living in the North Cascades before archaeological explorations carried out by Robert Mierendorf and other National Park Service personnel between 1987 and 1989. These explorations have been amplified by ongoing work. East of Ross Lake near the Canadian border and, to a lesser extent, on the west side of Ross near Little Beaver Creek, scientists found deposits of native tools, charred animal bones, and other indications of humans. These tools have been carbon-dated to 6458 B.C.—more than 8,000 years ago. In a steep, almost inaccessible area searchers also found a rock shelter, a natural overhang that had been enlarged using tools. Clearly the ancient people came specifically to the area to mine chert, a form of quartz, and make cutting tools, hammers, and such. Evidence indicates temporary, not permanent, occupation. It took trained eyes to spot the sites, for brush and trees have overgrown them and the earth itself has covered the artifacts (virtually all fragmented) with as much as five or six feet of dirt, requiring carefully executed archaeological excavation to unearth them. The finds were electrifying as the first positive evidence of prehistoric inhabitation of the Cascades.

For some reason most Native Americans left the remote mountains before the advent of white explorers. Accounts by Hudson's Bay fur trappers and that of Henry Custer (Heinrich Koster), who explored the North Cascades in 1857–59 as part of a boundary survey, indicate few encounters with Indians and few remains of human intrusion there—except for brush hunting shelters probably from the 1800s. Quite possibly the glaciers of the Little Ice Age (discussed in Chapter 1) discouraged exploration and hunting.

West of the Mountains: The Upper Skagit Tribes

From tribal historians we know that the Upper Skagit people were using the Skagit and Cascade River valleys for permanent residence and intermittent access to the high mountains for hunting, fishing, berrying, and wool gathering within the last few hundred years. In so doing they encountered the Lower Thompson bands, considered mortal enemies, coming into the Skagit River valley from the north. The Thompsons came to hunt, fish, and raid Upper Skagit settlements for blankets, dried fish, and potential brides. Some Skagits called them "stick Indians," a term that could mean people from the wilderness or Indians who were phantoms and could influence your life for evil or good. A tribal member who died in 1996 remembered fighting off raiding parties and asserted that he had killed at least six Thompsons. Nonetheless, tribal accounts indicate some peaceful communication between the two groups, too, with consensual intermarriage.

The Upper Skagits claimed as their territorial boundaries the lands lying roughly between today's Rockport on the west to the Okanogan–Chelan county lines on the east, and from the international border to a point somewhat south of the Skagit River near the Sauk. The lands were not sharply delineated but, in the Native American fashion, were areas that were visited regularly and considered a part of the tribe's hunting/fishing/gathering domain. Such loosely defined boundaries overlapped with the activities of their neighbors. Mount Baker was considered one of the guardian spirits of the Upper Skagit people; they called the volcano t'kuba or "snow all around." The slopes of the mountain were popular for gathering huckleberries, wild strawberries, and blackberries, just as they are today.

The Skagits lived in permanent homes, augmented by fishing and hunting camps where some structures might remain between visits. A "village" might consist of one or more longhouses, a ceremonial house, drying racks, smokehouses, houses reserved for young women celebrating puberty, sweathouses (although not numerous), and shelters strung along as much as a five-mile section—not a compact group of homes as Europeans called villages. Archaeologists only recently intensified their search for the village locations suggested by tribal historians and early explorers' accounts. Until 1995 only seventeen native sites had been recorded in the entire North Cascades National Park. Now 250 are recorded in the park territory alone—most detectable only to a trained eye. The most significant village of the upper valley was at the junction of the Sauk and Skagit Rivers near today's Rockport, but a bevy of others extended up the Cascade River valley beyond Marblemount and up the Skagit River to Newhalem. Beyond that no sites have been found and, other than hunting camps, probably did not exist due to the difficulty of traversing the Skagit River canyon.

The Skagits' name for themselves was merely *Hum-a-luh* or "the people." They were part of the coastal Salish grouping but spoke a different dialect from their Lower Skagit kinsmen, much as Bostonians sound different from San Franciscans. The nuances of the languages, though, were such that the Skagit language was unintelligible to the Chilliwacks or Chelans. Early trappers and settlers often referred to coastal Indians as "Siwash," possibly a corruption of the French word for savage (*sauvage*) or a variation on Salish. The word had a derogatory connotation. Although the Upper Skagits had their own language, slightly different from that of the lower bands, it is probable that many natives knew Chinook as well, the universal coastal trading language that has given us such commonly used words as potlatch and *chechacho*, and lesser known words such as *klahowya* (hello), *chikamin* (money), and *tillacum* (friend). Halfway between the ocean and the eastern plateaus of Washington, the Upper Skagits lived in a manner that borrowed from both—depending on salmon and steelhead for staple food like the coastal people, but amplifying their food sources by hunting. A few Indians kept horses, the better to traverse the mountain trails to trade with the eastern slope Indians.

Like their coastal neighbors the Upper Skagits traveled mostly by canoe. They crafted at least three kinds of canoes—the large shovel-nosed dugout, a smaller one- or two-man canoe, and a strange one that sloped downward at both ends, used for hunting waterfowl. The shovel-nosed dugout could hold ten to thirty-five people. It was hollowed from a cedar log and bent upward at both ends by steaming or soaking the wood in hot water. The canoe was easy to navigate on the swift rivers and to portage or drag over shallow sandbars. Small canoes were used for root-gathering, hunting, or errands, much as we might drive a car to shop. In fact, in the late nineteenth and early twentieth centuries the U.S. Postal Service hired Indians to carry the mail by canoe to upriver areas.

Less often crafted, the salt chuck canoe intended for ocean travel could hold an entire family. It had a broad beam and a raised, pointed bow to deal with the rougher water encountered on the Sound. The prow usually was decorated with a colored design topped by a figurehead (much like those of old sailing ships) of an animal or bird—perhaps one meaningful to the family of the owner. This seagoing version had a short mast, to support a sail if the winds were favorable.

A resurgence of interest in canoes and kayaks has sparked recreation of traditional designs, but most old canoes are seen only in museums. A few racing canoes at the Lummi Stommish races (which attract coastal competitors from great distances) are built by the old methods, using boiling water to shape the wood and a hand adz to smooth the surfaces. Some of these racing canoes are similar to the Tlingit, Haida, and Tsimshian war canoes in which warriors sped to and from the Puget Sound inlets to seize slaves and plunder the camps of Skagits and Lummis. Indeed, even after the advent of white settlers, Colonel Ebey, a government official from Port Townsend who lived across the water at Whidbey Island, was attacked and beheaded by the warlike northern warriors.

The Skagits harvested salmon and steelhead with seines across the river, by setting a net with one closed end in shallow water, or using dip nets of a unique design: two parallel handles were attached to a basketball-like hoop and net, and a third was attached to the back of the net. The handler simply scooped fish from the stream and dumped them out by pulling on the center handle. Individuals also speared fish with a three-pronged affair or placed a log across shallow streams so that a salmon leaping over the log would land on a dry-air platform to be picked off at the leisure of the fisherman. Fish to be eaten fresh were prepared in one of several ways: covered with wet moss and steamed in an ash pit; boiled in pots; cut into large fillets and baked almost upright adjacent to cooking fires; or cut into small slices and grilled over an open fire. The vast majority of the salmon or steelhead necessarily was preserved for later use by smoking or drying.

Hunters took their quarry with bow and arrow: the bow of yew or alder, the arrow a shaft of ironwood tipped by white stone. They also prepared deadfalls (holes covered lightly with branches) or drove deer over cliffs to their deaths. The hides were used to make clothing: buckskin in winter, doeskin in summer. According to June McCormick Collins in her book *Valley of the Spirits*, men often went naked if the weather permitted, but women wore long skirts of cedar bark or, more often, of wool. In winter men and women might wear hide garments with the fur inside, knee-length moccasins, gloves, and mink hats.

Like their coastal cousins, "high-class" Skagits flattened the heads of their infants to rise from the forehead to a peak. Men and women wore long hair parted in the middle and tied in a ponytail with a thong, although women also wore braids. Women lightly tattooed designs on their faces, arms above the wrist, and legs and ankles (a practice also prized by the Ainu of Japan's Hokkaido Island).

A definite class system existed, and families tended to marry their children to a mate of the same or higher class. Great value was placed on work, and the highest compliment a prospective bride's family could make about an aspiring groom was that he worked all the time. Marriages were arranged (although the children's wishes were considered) with regard to economic or social status and included marriages between younger men/older women or vice versa. While monogamy was preferred, polygamy was occasionally practiced. If a man had several wives, each had her own hearth and the man cohabited with each wife in turn.

Anthropologists declare that the Upper Skagits were unsurpassed in the quality of their baskets, used for cooking, carrying, and storage. They also knew about weaving long before the white man came. In the hot weather of early summer, goats rubbed themselves against bushes to get rid of their winter coats; the natives only had to gather the clumps sticking to the shrubbery of the mountain slopes. The Upper Skagits used the wool to weave their own blankets and traded wool or blankets for marine products garnered by their coastal relatives. Probably using the Acme Valley as a trade route, they also visited and mingled with the Nooksack Indians, whose territory was near the junction of the three forks of the Nooksack River.

Hostilities between the Upper Skagits and Lower Thompsons included resentment of the latter's gathering of goat wool from bushes in the Cascades before Skagits could get there. This animosity did not seem to extend to the natives east of the mountains, who were viewed as trading partners.

Although Catholic priests and missionaries worked among the people and converted many of them to Christianity, individuals were troubled by the conflict between Catholicism and the retention of their guardian spirits and other native beliefs. In the 1890s the Shaker Church became popular, partly because—although Christian in orientation— its doctrines did not require the Indians to relinquish their guardian spirits; instead, the powers of such spirits were transferred into the Shaker power of the individual. With some differences the Shaker Church embraces much of the ritual of the Protestant churches with Bible readings, hymns from Protestant hymnals, and so on.

The Upper Skagits originally had no governments or headmen as such. Each family was responsible for the behavior of its own members. When the United States government asked for chiefs to speak for the tribes, the Upper Skagit elected their first such leader *s'ab btik*, son of an Okanogan man who had come to live with the tribe in the late nineteenth century because his life was threatened by a shaman. The son was known as John Campbell or Chief Campbell and his offspring inherited the title.

According to pioneer Otto Klement, in 1873 the valley supported about two thousand Indians and sixty settlers. The two thousand may have included Indian people from upriver to the coast. Probably spread by visiting Hudson's Bay Company trappers or natives from the east, devastating epidemics of measles and smallpox in the 1840s—and as early as 1780—had decimated their former numbers. Trader N. E. Goodell, who established a store at Goodell's Landing (Newhalem) in 1879, estimated the native people of the Upper Skagit (above Rockport) at about 400. He formed warm friendships with the people and two chiefs, John Campbell and John Quwoitkin, and wrote in a letter to his nephew that he had never seen a people who loved their homes or honored their ancestors more. Quwoitkin's home was about 200 feet long and 50 feet wide, constructed of cedar, and large enough to hold the whole tribe for potlatch (gift exchange) festivals. The home also served as a council chamber, a place to which Goodell was summoned for advice during his trading post days.

The only threat to peace between the white settlers and the Upper Skagits came around 1880 (exact date unknown). Tension arose over the murder of an Upper Skagit Indian by another tribal member and the arrest of a suspect by white authorities, removing jurisdiction of the crime from control of the tribe. With bad timing, a white surveyor appeared to mark the boundaries claimed by the Upper Skagits. The tribe perceived this as a prelude to opening their lands to homesteaders. The surveyor's compass was smashed and tribal authorities ordered him to leave. A few days later the tribe contacted all white settlers and threatened them with harm if they did not leave as well. At a council between the two sides no agreement was reached, and the Indians protested formally about the breach of their autonomy, since they had never ceded their lands to the United States nor signed a treaty. (Chief Campbell had attended the meetings that resulted in the Point Elliott Treaty of 1855, but did not sign the treaty; hence, later in the twentieth century, the tribe had to be re-established by appeal. Alice Washington, the first Upper Skagit Indian to graduate from Concrete High School, was instrumental in gaining federal recognition for the Upper Skagits as a distinct tribe in 1974.)

Indians "drew the line" near the Pressentin Ranch at Birdsview with one hundred manned canoes. Summoned by the white government, a company of soldiers under Colonel Simmons came from Vancouver, Washington, to put down what loomed as an armed conflict. Upon

After emerging from the Gorge, the Skagit River meanders through the lovely Skagit Valley (Photo by JoAnn Roe).

seeing the soldiers the Skagits fled. In a later council they reiterated their position to Simmons, who told them there would be trouble if they harmed the settlers and recommended that they lay the problem before the Department of Justice. Instead, most of the Indians moved into more remote upriver areas. Somewhat later, under Chief Wa-wit-kin, the tribe appealed to Territorial Judge Roger S. Green for relief. He asked them to apply to Congress but they may not have done so; the record is unclear. In 1892, some specific allotments were made by the United States but refused by the Upper Skagits on the basis that they already owned the land. After establishment of the Washington National Forest in 1897, including lands claimed by the Upper Skagits, many tribal members applied for allotments within the forest. Most were refused but, in 1909, allotments were made on the Sauk River instead. Some Skagits moved there, built traditional houses, and continued their aboriginal practices. Others essentially joined the world of the white man.

The great majority of the agreeable, adaptable Upper Skagits readily adjusted their lifestyles to that of the white settlers beginning in the late 1800s. By the middle 1900s aboriginal life patterns were declining. The Upper Skagits wore western-style clothing, lived in ordinary houses, and worked at the same jobs as those of their white neighbors, especially in the logging industry. Ken Cuthbert, a tribal member and retired logger, remembers the closeness of the Indian people in earlier days, though. "We would get together at the old Rockport village for ballgames and pow-wows regularly." An upsetting chapter in their lives paralleled that of other native tribes, when their school-age children were forced to relinquish their own language and ways and frequently were "banished" to boarding schools. They returned home or entered the western world as educated persons but were left bereft of much of their native culture, until the late twentieth century renaissance of interest in Native American traditions.

In 1995, the Upper Skagit tribe opened Harrah's, an attractive casino on Bow Hill along Interstate 5, an enterprise calculated to improve the tribal economy. About 700 persons are registered members of the tribe today. The tribe's history and spiritual customs are being resurrected and taught, so that tomorrow's children will have knowledge of their culture despite living in the modern world.

East of the Mountains: The Methows, Okanogans, Moses, and Colville Federated Tribes

Although anthropologists previously believed that Native Americans did not live permanently in the foothills of the Cascades above Winthrop (within the scope of this book), recent discoveries of depressions identified as pit house sites, which were winter dwellings, refute the theories. The presence of natives was mentioned in an article in the *Methow Valley Journal* of October 28, 1937. Clint Hanks, Del Morris, and "Amsey" Clothier of the maintenance crew for the U.S. Forest Service found cedar stumps about two miles above Lost River cut all the way around the tree in a manner consistent with the use of old Native American tools. By counting the rings of the stumps the men estimated the cuts were made at least 500 years ago. Since Indians built cedar canoes as long as eighteen feet, perhaps the cedars were cut for this purpose. The men also found a few cedars of a different species from those presently growing, shorter and with larger butts, giving rise to speculation that the old stumps were from a time of more precipitation than that falling today. Not far distant was a tree burned as if used as a signal.

More horse-oriented than the Indians of the western slopes, the Methows, Okanogans, and others traveled westward over the Cascade Pass Trail to trade their wares for clams, shells, the esteemed Skagit wool blankets, and other products. The trading trail essentially came up the Twisp River, connected with trails to Cascade Pass and down the Cascade River to today's Marblemount. (See Chapter 3 for more on this route.)

The eastern Washington tribes traditionally drove their extensive horse herds up the Methow Valley for summer grazing, then burned the valley as they left in the fall to discourage weeds and shrubbery. They left their names on prominent points. The Indian name for Lost River was *Appiow* (phonetic spelling) meaning "the river that enters the wall." The name *Methow* is believed to mean "plenty," *Mazama* is Indian or Spanish for "goat," and the town of Twisp is derived from *twistsp*, or the sound of a buzzing wasp or yellow jacket.

The Methow Valley constituted the main portion of the Chief Moses Reservation until it was sold back to the government in 1886 and opened for homesteading. A writer known only as "Old Flint" wrote in the Bellingham *American-Reveille* of September 1, 1907, that his horseback party had encountered an Indian called Methow George on Early Winters Creek, where he, his wife, and their children were hunting deer, drying jerky, and tanning hides. Methow George later lived at Twisp; he moved to the Colville Reservation in disgust after he learned he would have to pay taxes on his Methow homestead but could have free land on the reservation.

Until the mid-1900s families of Native Americans continued to come to the Winthrop area and the upper Methow Valley to dig camas bulbs, dry fish, or pick berries, seasonal cycles of life that had existed as long as any could remember.

Life changed as the tribes adopted many of the white man's ways. In Okanogan County Indians and whites were and are heavily intermarried and have lived peacefully side by side most of the time, on and off the reservation.

3. EARLY CROSSINGS

The Ross Expedition

The first known crossing by whites of the area near the North Cascades Highway was made by Alexander Ross in 1814. Ross was assigned to Fort Okanogan, located on the Columbia River near present-day Brewster, a fur collection point and outpost for the North West Company (which later merged with the Hudson's Bay Company). Here the canoe brigades from Fort Vancouver put into shore and formed pack trains to bring supplies north through the Okanagan Valley of Canada and on to Alexandria and Prince George. Other canoe brigades continued up the Columbia River as far as the Big Bend in Canada, a point where the river makes a hairpin turn from a northwesterly to southerly flow. There the canoeists proceeded on foot or horseback across the mountains north of Jasper to resume a canoe journey to Hudson's Bay or Red River (Winnipeg).

The canoe trip from Fort Vancouver was dangerous. The Columbia was filled with rapids and blocked by a waterfall at The Dalles (Celilo Falls). Voyagers had occasional run-ins with hostile Indians. Ross wondered if there were some other way to saltwater, a path that would be a supply line for ships from Puget Sound instead of Fort Vancouver.

Ross queried the local chief Red Fox about Cascade trails. Red Fox said he had been many times to the "Great Salt Lake," that the route was almost due west, but the trail had not been used in recent years. Nonetheless, with one Indian guide who had been on the trail many years earlier, plus two Indian companions, Ross set out in July 1814 to cross the mountains.

The party followed the Methow River until, tiring of its many loops and backwashes, Ross struck out across the foothills around Hunter Mountain and continued roughly parallel to but south of the Methow River until he struck the Twisp River. The Indian guide recognized the river and led Ross uphill to cross Twisp Pass, then through snow-choked Copper Pass south of Liberty Bell Mountain. Taking a path parallel to today's Highway 20, the four men reached Bridge Creek, turned south probably as far as the Stehekin River, then west to the steep switchbacks of the eastern face of Cascade Pass. As they entered the high country of Cascade Pass, the trees were dense and tall, almost shutting out the sun, and the men often lost the faint trail. The party struggled over large boulders and through underbrush.

The Indian guide was curious about Ross's compass and asked why he kept looking at it. Ross replied that it was the white man's guide, that it had hands that pointed to the right trail. The Indian asked, "If you have a guide of your own, why do you want me?" Ross held up his double-barreled gun in one hand and his single-barreled rifle in the other and asked which was better, one or two. The guide readily agreed that the double-barreled gun was better, and Ross said, "The same with guides. If one fails, we have the other."

Little did he know that the assertion soon would prove true. Within a few days Ross and his party, chilled and tired, reached a crest where the streams flowed west. Weakened by exposure and fatigue, the guide fell ill. After two days in camp without any improvement in the guide's condition, Ross decided he must either go forward or return to Okanogan before supplies ran out or the cold of the high country overwhelmed them all. After two slow days of travel, the sick guide could go no farther. Ross left one companion to care for him in camp (around Mineral Park), while he and the other Indian forged ahead, marking their trail clearly for the return trip. After two grueling days of travel, they came into an area of gentler terrain with open woods, probably fairly close to Marblemount. Fate intervened. Ross wrote in his account that there was a terrifying and mysterious noise like a heavy body falling from a great height. An ominous cloud and a roaring came closer, and trees crashed to the ground like saplings. The hurricane passed less than a quarter mile distant, wreaking havoc on the trail ahead. The Indian pleaded with Ross to go back. The next morning the Indian was missing and Ross had no choice but to retreat. When he caught up with his party, he found a second Indian ailing, sick from overexertion and exposure. There was nothing to do but hasten back to Okanogan, two weeks distant. The guide told a disappointed Ross that, from his description of the terrain, he probably had been within four days of the ocean. Ross was later transferred and did not return to his explorations in the pass.

Rail Surveys

In 1853, General George B. McClellan was ordered to explore the North Cascades for a railroad route, but he never crossed the range. He traveled north and south along both sides of the mountains, going as far north as Lake Okanagan in Canada on the eastern slope. He planned to canoe as far as Bellingham on the western side but was turned back north of the Snohomish Valley by a winter storm carrying high winds and snow. From consultations with Indian people and earliest settlers he wrote in his report to the U.S. government:

> Upon an attentive consideration . . . I think it will be very evident that there is but one pass through the Cascade range from the Columbia to the northern boundary—that of the main Yakima—that is at all practicable for a railway; nor am I aware of any reason for believing any to exist between that boundary and Thompson's River.
>
> —House Doc. 129, Serial 736, pp. 147 ff.

As early as 1870, D. C. Linsley combed the ridges between Lake Chelan and Cady Pass, looking for a logical place to build a new railroad to Puget Sound for Northern Pacific. He was followed over the next decades by several other surveying parties who routinely used the Skagit River to access the foothills, then turned into the Sauk River to gain further mileage into the North Cascades Range. Finally John F. Stevens discovered Stevens Pass in 1890 for the Great Northern Railroad and the rail surveys dwindled.

Other Explorations

Henry Custer explored the extreme North Cascades quite thoroughly between 1857 and 1859, while off duty from officially surveying the forty-ninth parallel. He worked overland about as far south as the Pickett Range, and took one trip down the Skagit River as far as today's Ross Dam.

In 1858 gold was discovered along the Fraser River. In an effort to get to the gold diggings, miners bushwhacked across Whatcom County with its towering trees or trekked up the Columbia and Okanogan Rivers and turned to attempt a straight-line course for the Fraser. That same year a pair of prospectors, A. S. Buffington and J. K. Tukey, explored the

Skagit River and were never heard of again. Also in 1858, the San Francisco newspaper *Daily Alta of California* ran a story about a party of sixteen miners bound for the gold rush who were attacked by Indians somewhere near Palmer Lake northwest of Omak, but escaped overland toward Winthrop to regroup. Two of the miners, Charles Bubb of Santa Clara, California, and John McCartney of Fort Wayne, Indiana, struck out in a northwesterly direction toward the Fraser, a course that took them into the Hart's Pass and Pasayten Wilderness regions. They wandered in snow and cloudy weather for days, ran out of food, and were obliged to eat roots, moss, and leaves. On the seventh day the weather cleared. They got their bearings, killed a poor little bluejay for sustenance, and kept going. Along the way they captured a fawn for food and struggled onto the gold trail east of Hope (probably the Coquihalla area), one more recorded—if unscheduled—crossing of the North Cascades.

Otto Klement and a small party traveled over the Cascade Pass route, searching for gold in the upper Skagit and on to the Methow River in 1877, returning later to the upper Skagit and Ruby Creek area to strike gold (see Chapter 4).

The Pierce Expedition

The next official exploration (and really the last except for later highway survey parties) was precipitated by the confrontation (see Chapter 2) between the Upper Skagit Indians and surveyors. The U.S. Army worried that perhaps the Upper Skagits might enlist the assistance of the eastern Washington tribes and wage a full-scale uprising. Indeed, the Upper Skagits had sent emissaries to eastern Washington but were rebuffed.

Lt. Henry H. Pierce was assigned to assess the condition of any trail from west to east. He left Fort Colville on August 1, 1882, accompanied by 1st Lt. George B. Backus, First Cavalry; Alfred Downing, Topographical Assistant; seven enlisted men; a packer; and Joseph LaFleur, guide and interpreter. Downing proved to be a wonderful artist and left a collection of sketches of the North Cascades that are probably the first depictions ever of the range. Pierce himself proved to be a capable writer, colorfully describing the terrain.

After an uneventful trip to the Methow Valley, Pierce hired a Chelan Indian guide to lead them to the headwaters of Lake Chelan. Ascending through the valley Pierce's party marched along the Twisp River trail. Nearing the high country around Little Bridge Creek, Pierce grew lyrical about the scenery, writing:

> To the south, the expansive slopes of the nearer mountains were covered with native grasses among the pines: at intervals, the receding uplands

forming beautiful, semi-circular, lawn-like areas along the river's edge. To
the north, the mountains, less prominent and less thickly wooded, were
frequently broken by jutting ledges to shift the monotony of the scene.
—Pierce's original manuscript dated September 30, 1882

And later as the peaks of the Cascade Range appeared, he wrote:
[Reynolds Mountain 8,512 ft.] Its vast proportions, sharply outlined
against the sky, assumed the form of some quaint temple of worship, with
its pointed gables, groined, dark-ribbed central dome, and shining roof.

As the party approached War Creek Pass, the guide seemed uncer-
tain as to the route. The men encountered a pair of prospectors and an
Indian guide named Captain Jim, who argued strenuously with Pierce's
Chelan guide Swa-u-lum about his planned approach. After a day's
dangerous and difficult ascent during which two pack animals tumbled
down the slope and had to be abandoned (though alive), Pierce apparently decided to accept Captain Jim's directions and made it safely over
War Creek and Purple Passes. From there the view of Lake Chelan was
breathtaking. Pierce wrote:
As we stood upon the lofty ridge—almost like the edge of a knife-blade,
scarcely a span separating the opposite declivities—and gazed westward
from a height of seven thousand feet above sea-level . . . At our feet, re-
posed [Lake] Chelan, in color like an artificial lake of very thick plate glass
deep-set in its frame-work of eternal bronze.

The party descended through thickets of underbrush to the Stehekin
River and turned toward Cascade Pass, passing Rainbow Falls. On August 23, 1882, they camped near the junction of the river and Bridge
Creek (the Pacific Crest Trail crosses there today). Thereafter, Pierce's
party followed essentially the same trail as today's approach to Cascade
Pass. En route they met the same prospectors again, who reported one
of their horses had tumbled to its death from the path. Disregarding
the prospectors' admonitions not to take the pack animals, Pierce's party
gained the summit north of Pelton Creek without mishap. LaFleur
scouted the pass approach and declared it out of the question to bring
pack animals farther. Except for three saddle mounts, he sent the pack
animals to the prior night's camp near Basin Creek, while Pierce, Downing, Backus, and the party's doctor, George F. Wilson, spent a miserable
night without food huddled under a tree, feet to a smoldering campfire,
dampened by sleet that later turned to snow.
In the morning the four men decided to press on, after ordering all
other men and animals at Basin Creek back to Fort Colville. Pierce's

party (accompanied by LaFleur) struggled on to a better camp higher on the pass, noticing outcroppings of gold or silver. On August 27 they descended westward into better weather but through tall cedars and occasional patches of nasty devil's club. Pierce commented that the trees were as "straight as gun barrels and without a knot for at least a hundred feet."

On August 30 the party halted at the junction of Boulder Creek and the Cascade River to consider the risks of fording the river, deep, swift and foaming among boulders. After discarding the idea of making a footbridge by felling a huge tree, the party risked the ford. Backus and LaFleur narrowly escaped death: LaFleur abandoned his horse in midstream and was forced to swim. When he had recovered from his chill, LaFleur went on ahead. He returned with the joyful news that the Skagit River was near, and he had found an Indian family willing to transport the party downriver by canoe.

On September 1, 1882, Pierce and his men traveled seventy-five miles down the sometimes turbulent river in the capable hands of the Indians to disembark at Sterling, a logging camp between today's Sedro-Woolley and Burlington. Fortified by good, hot meals and a night's sleep, the party went on to Mount Vernon and eventually by steamer to Seattle.

Pierce's 295-mile expedition was the most complete to that time. Considering the steepness and difficulties of the trail, Pierce reported, it was not probable that the Cascade Pass Trail would be used by war parties to cause trouble for the settlers of the Sound. Nor was it necessary to construct a military road through the mountains.

The report, published in 1883 in a federal government publication, elicited interest from railroad builders, miners, and settlers.

4. GOLD FEVER

The Fraser River and Barkerville gold rush that exploded in 1858 kindled belated interest in the North Cascades as a possible bonanza site. In 1877, Skagit Valley resident Otto Klement, together with John Rowley, Charles von Pressentin, John Duncan, and Frank Scott, set out to explore Cascade Pass and the upper Skagit. At the Skagit River Gorge above Newhalem they made crude sluices and worked the river, gaining some fine placer gold but no indications of any upriver lode. Nonetheless, they packed their tools over Sourdough Mountain (named because one of the party spilled some of his sourdough starter) to Ruby Creek and the Skagit River. In late fall they were driven out of the mountains by snow, but had found sufficient color that most returned in February 1878, and again in early 1879. There they found the Albert Bacon party on Ruby Creek; by April the Bacon party had taken out gold dust worth $1,500 and Rowley's party had mined about $1,000. When the latter returned to Mount Vernon for supplies later in April, the good news could not be hidden and prospectors swarmed into the upper Skagit River country, spreading out along the creeks and rivers: Thunder, Ruby, Slate, Granite, Canyon, Mill, Beaver, and others.

The Ruby Creek Boom

The miners formed the Ruby Creek Mining District, adjoining the later Slate Creek District, and elected George Sawyer as the recorder.

Platted while still under twenty feet of snow, Ruby City never was more than a collection of shacks plus the Ruby Creek Inn and restaurant (on a site now beneath Ross Lake). Prospectors filed ninety-six claims on Granite Creek and thirty on Thunder Creek. The Skagit Mining Company organized in May 1880 for $1 million to develop mining properties.

The main problem for the prospectors was the distance from a supply point. Businessmen in Bellingham, Mount Vernon, and even Port Townsend schemed as to how they could create a trail or supply the miners by boat. Would-be suppliers in Seattle even suggested using hot-air balloons to transport supplies. At one point Dan Harris of Bellingham drove three head of cattle via the Nooksack Trail into the Ruby Creek region, but when he arrived, the starving miners had no cash. When the mood turned ugly, Harris left one animal as a peace offering and prudently departed. Miner John R. Ryan reported that supplies arriving at the camps sold for huge prices: five dollars for a sack of flour, thirty cents a pound for bacon, ten dollars for rubber boots.

Just two routes awaited the incoming prospector: the foot trail to Ruby Creek over the dangerously narrow ledge trail through the Skagit Gorge, impassable for pack stock at first, or the Nooksack Trail from Bellingham to Hope and back south on the Skagit River. Miners entering the Cascade Pass area went up the Cascade River and veered off toward Thunder Creek or came in from the Skagit Gorge. In July 1880 the hundred-ton steamer *Chehalis* went farther upstream on the Skagit than anyone ever had before, to Goodell's Landing (Newhalem). The fare from Mount Vernon and vicinity was twelve dollars round trip, later reduced to eight dollars.

But at Goodell's the miner's easy approach ended and he was faced with the awful gorge. One scoundrel, a Captain Randolph, built a house across a narrow portion of trail, demanding a toll to pass through. Randolph and his structure mysteriously disappeared, though. . . . A particularly bad point in the trail was at Devil's Corner (later dubbed Devil's Elbow), a ledge that lies directly above Tunnel No. 1 on today's highway; an overhanging rock there required a series of ladders to enable prospectors to pass.

Nonetheless, for about two years a lively gold rush to the upper Skagit contributed to the development of the valley's towns. By March 15, 1880, while snow still lay four feet deep at Ruby Creek, men were busy prospecting and more were coming. A traveler in April reported that he found the entire length of Ruby and Canyon Creeks claimed, as well as claims on Granite, Mill, and Slate Creeks.

Before year's end the boom was over. The LaConner newspaper *Puget Sound Mail* reported in October 30, 1880, that "the Ruby gold rush

Prospectors traveling eastward through the Skagit Gorge resorted to scaffolding to traverse the treacherous area. They dubbed their route the "Goat Trail" (Photo courtesy of Whatcom Museum of History and Art, Bellingham).

was over," and that it had been a failure. The men who had come to the Skagit in this brief gold rush dispersed swiftly, some to better prospects at Barkerville.

Established Mines

A few determined men, more solvent and able to bring heavier equipment into the area, continued to work the upper Skagit. Jack Durand worked the Colonial Mine on Colonial Creek, a tributary of the Thunder. John Rouse, L. S. Stevens, George Rowse, and F. Reese found a quartz ledge purportedly rich in gold and silver on the Cascade River in 1885. Such companies mined the land, not the river (placer mining). They were the forerunners of a substantial boom in the late 1880s and 1890s on both sides of the North Cascades, mostly north of today's North Cascades Highway, but also along the old Cascade Pass Trail, especially in Horseshoe Basin above Lake Chelan.

One lasting boom was begun by an intelligent prospector named Alex Barron, who reasoned that, with so much free gold in the streams, a mother lode must exist. Tracing the gold ever higher through seemingly impassable country, Barron struck a bonanza in 1892 on a quartz ledge off today's Hart's Pass. He called his discovery the Eureka Mine. More of a prospector than a serious businessman, Barron sold his claim to the Eureka Mining Company of Anacortes, Washington, for a reported $50,000–$80,000 and took an extended vacation. The worth of this claim was emphasized in 1893 by the sending of a 400-pound chunk of gold-bearing quartz to the World's Columbian Exposition in Chicago. It was transported from the high country by canoe down Slate, Canyon, and Ruby Creeks, and then down the Skagit River.

Hampered always by poor trails and distance from smelters (either Idaho or Tacoma), miners swarmed through the mountains, trying industriously to make a fortune. From 1894 to 1937, 2,812 claims were filed in the upper Skagit area alone. The more promising mines included the Tacoma, Goat, Indiana, Illinois, Mammoth, Mountain Goat, and Anacortes. Near the rich strike of the Eureka was a forest of claim stakes. Nuggets worth twenty dollars or more were found in several places.

The huge problem of transporting machinery into the high mountains continued to hamper development of the claims. No practical trail existed beyond Newhalem, nor was the Dewdney Trail from Fort Hope and south on the Skagit River very useful. The best prospect was from the east through the Methow Valley, and in the spring of 1895, Col. Thomas Hart, an engineer/surveyor with an option on the Mammoth Mine, contracted for and swiftly began work on a twenty-two mile wagon road from Robinson Creek to the mines.

Bridge Creek and Cascade mining districts (Photo courtesy of BBIC map collection at the Center for Pacific Northwest Studies, Western Washington University, Bellingham, Washington).

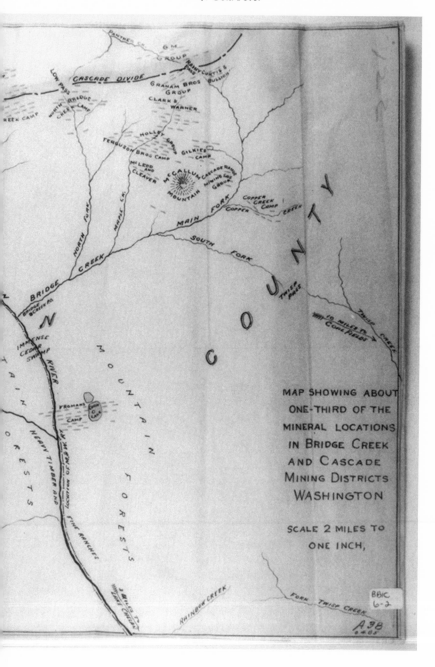

Meanwhile, Daly & Clark of Montana hired men to probe the Mammoth Mine by tunnel but, after spending $100,000 in development, concluded the assays were not cost-effective and stopped work. Apparently, Hart was out of luck but he was determined to build a wagon road to the site. He turned the project over to Charles Ballard, a pioneer prospector and engineer who later would become a major mining figure, to complete. With assistance from engineer Melville Curtis, Ballard finished an adequate if treacherous road by 1903—treacherous because along one rocky section, the road was literally pinned to the cliff, hanging over a chasm. After an entire pack train fell off the trail to disaster, the spot became known as Dead Horse Point. In the village of Winthrop, meanwhile, special narrow-gauge wagons were fabricated to negotiate the Hart's Pass Road, to be pulled by horses linked in tandem. Often the equipment was broken down into sections for transport.

The road served the mining area well, however, and although much improved by the late twentieth century, it still poses a challenge for modern vehicles over the rocky, narrow section.

In addition to roadbuilding, in 1897 Charles Ballard took an option on the Mammoth Mine near the Eureka, installed a stamp mill and other facilities, and reportedly took out $5,000 to $6,000 a month in gold. Changes of owners and extensive development work on the original strike (the Eureka Mine) had delayed any real "take" from that site, but in 1898 Charles D. Lane of San Francisco built a sawmill, ten-stamp mill, and staff buildings there. Investing about $100,000 in heavy equipment, he excavated into the ledge more than 100 feet and found very rich sylvanite ore, some showing as much as 60 percent gold. The Eureka began to produce $17,000 to $18,000 a month in gold; by 1899, 100 men were employed under the supervision of C. W. Tozier.

Ballard's Mammoth Mine realized $397,000 from 1898–1901, and other miners took advantage of gold-bearing ore that lay near the surface, easy to process. A visitor, D. B. Schaller, said that about seventy men were working for mining companies in the upper Slate Creek at wages of $80 to $100 per month. Translate that salary range into late twentieth century terms and the workers were getting rich, too.

The boom at the Whatcom–Okanogan County border, however, began to fade shortly after 1900, when gold near the surface had been harvested, and the lure of the newly discovered Yukon gold took miners away. Not so with those around the Eureka strike, though. The *Methow Valley News* of April 1, 1904, quoted Charles Ballard as saying: "A few days ago we struck in the mine about eight feet in the foot wall a parallel ore body four feet wide and carrying high grade values. We have drifted about twenty feet on it, and it is holding its own."

Wreckage at Eureka Mine site, Barron, Hart's Pass, 1992 (Photo by JoAnn Roe).

The following year the Eureka Consolidated Mining Company was incorporated by Charles and Anna Ballard and James Cady with capital stock of $1.5 million and a business address at Barron, Washington. The author believes that, at this time, Ballard's company also acquired the Eureka and changed its name to the Bonita Mine. (Tracing the fate of mining companies through corporate records is often a tangled saga.) Ballard faced the ongoing problem of transporting reduced ore to the distant smelters and, in a 1926 newspaper interview, claimed that in the early century he sent ten tons of concentrate to the Tacoma Smelter, received a check for $660 and had spent half that for mere transportation. Exactly when Ballard ceased operating is unclear, but 1915 records show the mine owner as William Brown of Everett.

During the Hart's Pass era the town of Barron boasted as many as 1,000 people in fairly permanent cabins. Serving their needs were

Old mine entrance at site of the Eureka Mine, Barron, Hart's Pass, 1992 (Photo by JoAnn Roe).

saloons, a dance hall, at least one restaurant, a post office, hotel, assay buildings, and others. The original town of Barron straggled along the creek below the Eureka Mine site and outgrew the buildable land. It was relocated a short distance east of Bonita Creek near its junction with Slate Creek. Along both locations are remains of foundations and, at the second site, extensive sections of large-diameter piping that led from creeks to the Mammoth mill, built in 1905.

In addition to the Barron and Mammoth, the Chancellor Mine nearby was a significant site with a sawmill, a power house, and a flume two miles long to serve a 240-horsepower generator four feet in diameter that had been cast in two sections for transport. Nicholas Aall, later an engineer for Seattle City Light, supervised the installation. Despite the orderly approach to development, the Chancellor folded after only a year. Its dilapidated buildings and rusting generator stood for years, surrounded by debris.

Another major mine, the North American Mining and Milling Company, operated for a few years after 1903 at the site where Alex

Barron had found a "glory hole" worth $20,000 prior to the big strike at the Eureka. The North American, managed by John Siegfried, had forty claims, tunnels 175 feet into one, and ore resting in a heap awaiting transportation. In 1905 the company added a ten-stamp mill and a 5,000-foot tram to transport ore from the Columbia claim to the mill. Yet the considerable investment did not pay off.

The Ruby–Canyon–Slate–Mill Creek mining sites continued to yield gold but not enough to create millionaires or even to return costs to their owners. The bubble burst and companies left for more promising sites, often leaving tools, wagons, bedding, and clothing behind, as if the owners had vanished from some mysterious disaster. A visitor, Bill Lester, went into Barron in the 1920s—thirteen years after the exodus—

Wreckage of Chancellor Mine building, Hart's Pass (Photo by JoAnn Roe).

and found liquor bottles still sitting on the bar at a saloon, narrow-gauge wagons awaiting ore, machinery that seemed ready to operate, and boxes of ruffled dresses for dancing girls long departed.

Barron and its mine were reincarnated under various names several times as late as 1983, when Nature took charge with a massive avalanche that crushed the mill and equipment, even reaching old barracks and messhouses a short distance away. The two Barrons disappeared, piece by piece, and only the fading outlines of building structures or tent foundations remain. The site is in private hands today, behind a sturdy fence and managed by a caretaker.

North and east of Hart's Pass a gold rush began after 1886, when Chief Moses Reservation was dissolved, in the area around today's Conconully, especially concentrated around a precipitous settlement called Ruby (confusing to historians, because of the other Ruby near Skagit River). The activities there did not directly affect the North Cascades Highway, but one should be aware that the gold rush of the 1880s–1900s included all of the North Cascades.

Simultaneous with the Hart's Pass activity other hopefuls tried their luck around Ruby Creek, Thunder Creek, and Horseshoe Bend (Cascade Pass). At least thirty-eight claims were operated along Ruby Creek, with colorful names like Rubber Neck, Noodrat, and Paymaster. In 1906, the Ruby Creek Mining Company worked the gravel beds at the confluence of the Ruby and Skagit (just below the viewpoint for Ross Lake on today's highway), erecting a sawmill, cookshack, bunkhouse, and a four-mile wooden flume to bring water to a hydraulic plant; however, it went bankrupt before doing much work. That same year, C. B. Brown installed a Pelton water wheel and generator on Ruby Creek to serve several mines at once.

Thunder Creek, which today feeds into Diablo Lake near the Diablo campground, was probed as well. In its upper reaches it ties into the high mountains east of Cascade Pass, separated from the Horseshoe Basin–Upper Stehekin diggings by the Sawtooth Range: spectacular, glacier-covered peaks of 6,000 to 8,000 feet. Along Thunder were the Bornite, Standard Reduction, North Coast Mining & Milling Company, the British Mining Company with 654 claims—apparently part of the North Coast group—and the Skagit Queen, most lasting of them all. Despite its proximity to Cascade Pass, the Skagit Queen was supplied largely from Marblemount. The local packers, Glee Davis (whom the author interviewed in 1971) and Jerome Martin, had to travel the marginal Skagit Gorge trail with their pack animals. Davis remembered packing a super-heavy single block for a compressor by using a tripod to lower it onto his strongest mule, moving ahead a few hundred feet, stopping, lifting the load off for a period of time with the tripod, and then repeating the process. Martin once packed in a great length of continuous cable by putting one coil on the lead packhorse, running a length back to the second, then to the third, and so on. One can only shudder at the thought of the chaos had even one of the packhorses spooked. Davis also remembered that ice formed on the ledge trail, making it so slippery that they "lined" a horse across such stretches by tying a rope to its tail and another to its head.

Investors O. P. Mason, E. H. Kohlhase, and Robert A. Tripple incorporated the Skagit Queen Mining Company for $1 million on July 1, 1905, with offices in Seattle. Management constructed a substantial camp: bunkhouse, messhall, storehouse, powder house, a barn, and small outbuildings. A crew bored into the most promising claim, the Dude Ledge, for 113 feet, then took an assay showing $200 silver and $9 gold per ton, but the deposits pinched off.

One of the firm's most promising deposits was the Willis E. Everette claim that lay in the formidable wall of the Sawtooths, mostly in Chelan County. An early test indicated $113 silver per ton. Eight to forty feet wide and, at one point, 220 feet, the vein ran clear through the Sawtooth Range; however, there is no record indicating the vein ever was worked substantially. Glaciers in the area advanced to engulf mines in ensuing years.

A complex set of mergers and acquisitions resulted in the joining under single ownership of Skagit Queen Mine, Protective Mining Company, Skagit Queen Consolidated Mining Company, British Mining Company, and Standard Reduction and Development Company, finally resting in the hands of Thunder Creek Mining Company. The British Mining Company had thirty-one claims and four millsites on Thunder Creek, had laid more than 1,400 feet of twenty-inch pipe to operate its power source, and had drilled a 660-foot tunnel on its properties. Thunder Creek Mining Company worked conservatively across the Skagit Queen Creek from the Skagit Queen Mine, boasting only two bunkhouses, a shop, and a small crew—but they had drilled into the mountain far enough to install a short set of rails supporting ore cars, and assayed their ore at the Tacoma Smelter. As late as 1908, the company joined with North Coast to acquire water rights for a potential power plant, and combined as Puget Sound, Cascade and Chelan Railway Company to build a railway that never happened. After taking over the above companies—or outlasting them—the Thunder Creek Mining Company failed also, and all mining ceased.

In 1971 Thunder Creek's claims came into the hands of Gregg C. MacDonald, Natural Resources Development Corporation, just before

Above Horseshoe Basin looking toward Boston Glacier area, Cascade Pass (Photo by JoAnn Roe).

the formation of North Cascades National Park. MacDonald, in turn, sold the claims to Glenn A. Widing of Portland, who attempted to build a road to the old mines for development purposes. After a prolonged ten-year battle between Widing and the Department of the Interior that included a special appeal by a member of the North Cascades Conservation Council to the 94th Congress, House Interior and Insular Affairs Committee, and fervent articles about retaining the pristine nature of Thunder Basin, Widing sold his claims in 1982 to the U.S. Government. Claims on the western side of Cascade Pass met with the same disposition.

Claims east of Cascade Pass in Horseshoe Basin, near Doubtful Lake, and even on or under the Sahale Glacier, Boston Glacier, and so on, appeared on a Kroll Map of 1899 like a modern real estate plat—hundreds of mining claims neatly laid out. As in other areas of the North Cascades, the terrain and lack of practical transportation prevented the miners from attaining their dreams of wealth. What the early gold rush period did do was inspire businessmen and settlers on both sides of the North Cascades to search for a route to link the northern portions of Washington state—a quest that failed until 1972.

The Azurite Mine

Just one company along the North Cascades Highway environs proved to be profitable and long-lasting. Charles Ballard and his brother Hazard, once owners of the Mammoth/Eureka finds, did not cease looking for their bonanza. In 1915–16 they found the Azurite and in 1917 the Gold Hill on opposite sides of Majestic Mountain in Mill Creek Valley. The name "Azurite" came from the azure blue carbonate of copper ore visible at the surface. In 1918, the Ballards formed the Azurite Copper Company of Delaware and obtained some financial backing from East Coast financiers, evidently a modest amount, as Charles told a reporter eight years later that he could not develop the property until he could accumulate investment capital. He did hire a packer to haul a small crusher and concentrator to the site, enabling him to extract a bit of gold. In 1925, he reorganized the venture as Azurite Gold Company with himself as president and his brother Arthur as secretary. Hazard worked the Gold Hill Mine.

Charles developed a short lead into the mountain that he called the Discovery Tunnel, exposing a promising vein. On the strength of his showings, he obtained working capital and began serious mining. First he built a road (with help from others) twenty-six miles into his property from the old Hart's Pass Road, providing access for freighters with narrow-gauge wagons. Among the equipment brought in by pack train

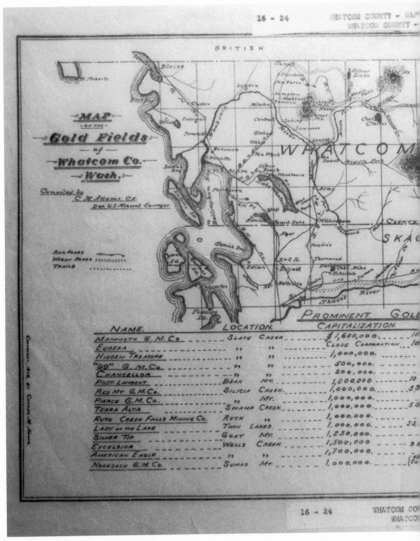

The gold fields of Whatcom County (Photo courtesy of BBIC map collection at the Center for Pacific Northwest Studies, Western Washington University, Bellingham, Washington).

(not wagons) were two diesel compressors, including a flywheel nine feet in diameter that had to be cast in three pieces and bolted together at the camp. The plan was to operate one compressor at a time, to avoid being without electricity during winter months. Soon after the first compressor was operative, it threw a rod and Ballard summoned a

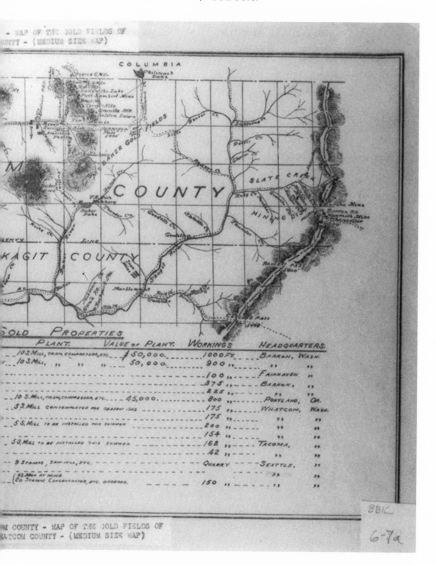

repairman from Pennsylvania to be transported to the mine by dogsled, an experience the easterner probably related to his grandchildren later in life. After 1929, working with George Therriault, Winthrop garage operator, Ballard developed continuous tracked, narrow-gauge tractors to pull the freight wagons. Later Therriault produced a company car as well, with a worm gear that permitted it to climb the steep roads; and for summer use Ballard ordered five trucks from International that had no fenders and extra-narrow axles.

Ballard invested in camp facilities, including a bunkhouse built partly into the mountain for protection against avalanches, a smithy, and mining buildings. In March 1930 he purchased a small smelter from the Mace Smelter Company of Denver that supposedly could process thirty tons of ore daily into a matte that could be transported easily to a major smelter. Workman Gordon Bainter said that the equipment failed the first summer, because the ore had a high iron content and the gold-bearing ore would not separate out properly.

After struggling along for another four years, Ballard was approached by American Smelting & Refining Company (ASARCO) and on January 2, 1934, concluded a sale of the Azurite: a $10,000 down payment plus a fifty/fifty sharing of net profits after ASARCO had recovered its initial investment, and a twenty-five-year lease of thirty-six lode claims and six mill sites. Charles Ballard died that same year, leaving his wife Anna as president. His brother Hazard sold his Gold Hill Mine and joined the Azurite firm.

Some Azurite workers brought their wives to live under primitive conditions during the balmy summer months, but the company required them to leave before snow fell. Mrs. Richard Horn, a new bride, kept a diary of her first stay at the Azurite. She arrived on the "puddle jumper," a specially equipped truck that brought light supplies. The puddle jumper was created by Harold Witte of Twisp for Charles Ballard. Starting with a used Model T Ford, Witte and George Therriault cut one foot from the front axle, shortened the front spring, cut off the back seat and made a makeshift truck bed, installed an extra water pump for better cooling and a Ruxtell axle to give an ample range of gears and lots of power, and added extra-powerful brakes and semi-balloon tires. The rig worked fine on the narrow, steep road to the Azurite, making the first trip from Robinson Creek in five hours. The return trip only took about two hours.

Horn wrote for August 2: "Eight switchbacks on Cady Mountain we had to back up to get around. Couldn't see far on account of the fog." The rest of that month's entries were fairly mundane, but on September 7, she wrote,

> Tonight the first standard gauge car that has ever been here drove in. Harvey Miller and Mrs. Dammann were in it. Created quite a sensation in camp. It is Henry's [Dammann] birthday and the cook made him an angelfood cake with one candle.

On September 23, she asked the mine manager if she could stay all winter but he said "nix." Mrs. Horn finally decided to leave on October 21, after several light snowfalls, but from that day through October 27 it stormed and snowed so badly that the puddle jumper could not leave.

An old miner's cabin at Canyon Creek still being used by prospectors in 1982 (Photo by JoAnn Roe).

At 8:00 A.M. on October 27, three tracked vehicles and one trailer set out for the Methow Valley. Mrs. Horn wrote that she rode on the trailer as far as Cady Summit and then on one of the tracked vehicles, that three to four feet of snow lay in their path.

> The puddle jumper was stuck in a slide near the Mammoth and they had to dig that out and tow it down to the Layout. Then the puddle jumper went ahead and some of us went on down to Robinson. We were 12½ hours from Azurite to Robinson Creek.

—Excerpts from "Azurite Bride's Diary," by Mrs. Richard Horn in the Winter 1974–75 *Okanogan County Heritage*

Mrs. Horn was fortunate to have made it out safely. The winter of 1934–35 was a bad one for snowslides. A large snowpack was topped by an icy crust when the temperature plunged to -38 degrees, followed in turn by another heavy snowfall of twelve feet or more. At the Azurite the extreme cold froze the water system to the cookhouse. After a snowfall of eight feet in eight hours, Charlie Graves, the cook, was dipping water from a stream when a slide came down, caving in the nearby supply shed and cascading over him. When workers realized he was missing, they correctly guessed his location and rescued him unhurt but cold and spouting colorful language.

Other men were not so lucky that winter. Two trappers were buried in their beds at a cabin on Trout Creek. About four miles from the Azurite on Mill Creek, a claim caretaker, 80-year-old Johnny Young, was nowhere to be found when Gordon Bainter and Dick Horn of Winthrop snowshoed in with supplies. They found his cabin partly smashed in, a half-eaten meal on the table, dirty dishes, and pans on the stove, all indicating that Young had left abruptly. Following his erratic trail, the men tracked him toward Slate Creek and found him dead and frozen, his feet still in his skis. A coyote had bitten him around the neck and head. Bainter and Horn tried to carry the corpse to his cabin but could not, so they tied old Johnny Young high in a tree beyond the reach of wild animals. Two weeks later when the weather abated, they returned to retrieve the body.

Operating the Azurite in winter at 5,080 feet was a challenge. All supplies either had to be dropped from an airplane or transported by dogsled. The Stonebreaker Company of Orofino, Idaho, was hired by ASARCO to maintain its supplies. Local mountaineer Ed Kikendall (who had learned to use dogs and sleds during a stint in Alaska) was designated as dog team operator, with brother Chuck assisting him. Ed had hauled in supplies by backpack during the winter of 1935–36, but the following year he acquired dogs and traveled up the west fork of the Methow River and over the Azurite Pass summit to the mine, a twenty-four mile trip. The dogs were crossbreds mostly, including huskies with some Irish setter blood. They were led by a remarkable animal with pale blue eyes. The dog loved attention but was too dignified to fawn over anyone. He just sat waiting, but most people were alarmed by his eerie eyes and thought he was dangerous.

Kikendall had a hectic first winter. Not only did he haul supplies and mail but he had to deal with not one, but three, cases of appendicitis. The son of Tacoma Smelter engineer Fred White was stricken on January 16, 1937, just after Kikendall had left for Winthrop. A day and a half later, Kikendall was met by a second team mushing uphill carrying Dr. E. P. Murdock—Azurite management had radioed to Winthrop that young White was in critical condition. Kikendall transferred the doctor to his own sled, and urged the team back to the mine. Murdock considered operating on the boy at the mine but discarded the idea as too dangerous, preferring to transfer him to the Okanogan hospital, about one hundred miles distant. Kikendall's weary team traveled downhill as fast as possible, with White and Murdock lashed to the dogsled. A racing team driven by Idahoan Ed Kimball met the party part way and delivered the doctor and his patient to a State Patrol car eight miles later. Officers sped to Okanogan via Pateros—the shorter Loup Loup road was blocked by snow. When Murdock, half-dead himself from exposure, finally operated on the boy, the appendix had ruptured and White died.

Forty-five days later, a second man, Howard James, had symptoms similar to White's. The mine manager assigned men to start out of the mountains as "dogs" lashed to a sled bearing James, while he summoned Kikendall. En route the sled went out of control on an icy slope and slid sidewise over a precipice with James still lashed to it. For a few awful moments he dangled while the men sat down in their tracks to stop his descent. Recovering their shaken patient, the men continued, met Kikendall, and sent James to the hospital, where he successfully recovered and eventually returned to work.

Another three weeks went by. On April 10, Azurite worker Chris Weppler became ill just after Kikendall had left for Winthrop, a nightmarish replay of the other two incidents. Worse yet, slides thundered down from early rains. Kikendall was feeding the dogs at his cabin when the telephone rang, summoning him back to the Azurite. Ed and his brother Chuck harnessed a double team and set a killing pace to meet the men bearing Weppler over the old Hart's Pass trail. The Kikendalls took Weppler as far as Dead Horse Point, where the snow gave way to mud and dirt but no vehicle was there to meet the team as promised. After waiting some hours, Ed decided Weppler was able to walk and supported him for a mile and a half down the trail to rescuers waiting at Robinson Creek. Weppler was rushed to the hospital for an appendectomy. He survived.

Life was not always that harrowing. By 1938 about seventy-five men worked year-round at the mine, often remaining on days off even in summer because of the distance to town. Management provided pool tables, a weekly movie, magazines, and good food. One Christmas an enterprising mechanic, Ray Allen, used an electric drill as a beater to produce Tom and Jerry drinks for all.

Azurite workers transported gold bullion each day to the Farmers

State Bank of Winthrop in cone-shaped blocks valued at $2,500. But by the end of 1938, the ore was petering out from the main Wenatchee Tunnel and new tunnels were not showing profitable amounts of gold. In 1939, pending a more thorough examination of the prospects, operations were suspended and the Azurite closed. From 1936 to 1939, the company had netted about $972,000, not enough to recover its $1 million investment. Management continued to probe for better and newer veins without success, and in 1942 the equipment was removed.

The site lay unworked until 1992, when present owner Joe Gray started to clean it up, removing carcasses of old machinery. His plan is to mine the tailings and eventually restore the site to return to the forest.

Current Mining Activity

When gold prices rose in recent years, some claimholders explored the feasibility of reopening operations at the old mines. But as indicated earlier, the Thunder Basin sites were acquired by the government and little activity in the Slate Creek area has ensued to this writing. The North Cascades still guard their secrets carefully. Most geologists agree that the gold is still there—but where? The fragmented and turbulent geologic history of the mountains caused gold deposits to lodge in bits and pieces, not in neat veins conducive to commercial extraction. Students and adventurers each year pan in the creeks and often can earn modest amounts over a laborious period of time, but the bonanza remains elusive.

5. A ROAD THROUGH THE MOUNTAINS

Throughout the period of gold prospecting, mining, and settling of the North Cascades country, men talked of building a pack trail, a wagon road, and later an automobile highway across the mountains. But until 1972 the only crossings were made on foot or on horseback, despite the irresponsible declarations of government officials and the media in 1897 that a good wagon road then existed across Cascade Pass.

The lack of adequate roads contributed sharply to the inability of gold miners to sustain a profitable operation. The high cost of hauling supplies and ore was the chief culprit in many mine failures.

Railroads were not the answer, either. As early as the 1850s surveying parties struggled over the ridges of the North Cascades. In 1881 the Northern Pacific established a route through Stampede Pass. Land speculators in the Methow Valley, Skagit Valley, and western Whatcom County followed the surveyors' progress closely and bold headlines fed rumors of "this town will be the one" and "buy land now in the path of progress." The *Methow Valley News* of October 1905 proclaimed that if all the railroads rumored to be built actually were, the settlers would have to move their homes up into the foothills to avoid being run over.

State Road Commission Surveys
In response to the need for roads, the Washington State Legislature established District No. 1 of the Road Commission for the North Cas-

cades in 1893. They appropriated the princely sum of $20,000, request-
ing matching funds from the counties for construction of a road from
Bellingham Bay to Marcus on the Columbia River. The legislature expected the road to touch at or near the Ruby Creek gold fields above
the Skagit Gorge. A three-man road commission was appointed to over-
see its development: John J. Cryderman, T. F. Hannegan, and a Mr.
Oliver.

Considering the difficulty of *walking* through the Skagit River gorge
above Newhalem, much less building a road, the commissioners sent a
survey party to investigate a possible route past Mount Baker to the
north/south Skagit River and Ruby Creek. With supplies to last one
month Banning Austin, E. P. Chace, H. Hall, and R. Lyle forced their
way up the north fork of the Nooksack River to Glacier Creek on horseback, then proceeded on foot to explore Austin Pass at the head of Wells
Creek and the Ruth Creek valley to Hannegan Pass.

None of the routes seemed promising except possibly Hannegan
Pass, then Whatcom Pass, and down Beaver Creek to the Skagit River
and eventually Ruby Creek. The westsiders promptly began to scrape
out a route toward Mount Baker. The road terminated two miles short
of Hannegan Pass at a total cost of only $57 a mile—well, maybe not a
road, but at least a passable trail.

Meanwhile, the eastsiders in Okanogan County had no money at
all toward their proposed $1,000 contribution to the road, but they
built (partly with volunteers, partly private donations) a significant
portion of trail toward Cascade Pass, and were able to build up the
Twisp River to the summit at a maximum of 16 percent grade with no
switchbacks. However, one wonders where the two trails would ever
have met (see map on pages 52–53). Political chicanery sank the effort after all, leaving two partial roads that ended in the middle of
nowhere.

A new survey by westsiders resulted in the declaration that the
concept of a road to Ruby would be scrapped. Miners reacted angrily to
the news, and businessmen in Bellingham produced sufficient donations
to send still another surveyor into the mountains, hoping for a positive
report, but engineer P. D. McKellar returned to concur with the past
surveyors' opinions.

At this same time the State Road Commission made a less politically sensitive study of a route across the Cascades via the Skagit
Valley. B. M. Huntoon of Bellingham, an experienced surveyor and
mountaineer, set out with a man named Harry on July 7, 1894, up the
south fork of the Nooksack River and east toward Baker Lake over a
rather high-altitude path similar to today's Forest Service Trail #3725.

Even in July the snow was three to four feet deep in places, and at one summit twelve feet deep! Nonetheless, Huntoon felt an eastbound road was feasible and continued his explorations as far as Baker Lake. Upon descending into Birdsview to replenish supplies, Huntoon wrote in his diary that no two people agreed, but most felt it was possible to get through the mountains around Baker Lake "someplace."

Along Baker Lake Huntoon stumbled while getting off a makeshift raft and impaled his kneecap on a hand pick fastened to the outside of his pack. Discounting the injury, Huntoon and Harry pressed on to the ranch of Bion H. Chadwick, but was forced to stop there as Huntoon could not bend his knee. Chadwick was a bear trapper and had rendered gallons of evil-smelling bear's oil, a remedy he swore by for wounds; he smeared it on Huntoon's knee, it killed the growing infection, and Huntoon was able to travel in a few days.

He and Harry decided to try to find Cryderman in the Austin Pass area. They ascended Swift Creek to the pass, where they found a blazed tree marked "May 1893" left by Austin the prior year. The two men continued down the Nooksack River along a route similar to today's Mount Baker Highway and found Cryderman's party about three miles below Nooksack Falls. Huntoon's survey, however, proved to be useless.

The State Road Commission was determined. They sent yet another survey party into the Cascades to explore a path eastward from Marblemount. There were three choices: up the Skagit Gorge to Ruby Creek and eventually over Hart's Pass; up the Skagit Gorge to Thunder Creek and then aim toward intercepting the eastsiders' rudimentary Twisp trail; or proceed along the time-honored Cascade Pass trail of Ross, Pierce, and prospectors, despite its formidable grade (almost a sheer descent that would require a tunnel or switchbacks) on the east side facing Lake Chelan.

To encourage the first choice, Skagit citizens offered their time with pick and shovel; the ladies of Anacortes gave fund-raising dinners to come up with $500 to buy blasting powder; and Albert Zabel of Hamilton donated his stagecoach to transport workers to the scene—all this so the trail could be widened for pack horses, at least. The citizens completed a six-foot-wide horse trail, despite the treacherous conditions of the gorge, that ascended along the north side of the Skagit River, then crossed to the south side on a new bridge short of the Devil's Elbow. It continued about four miles upstream to Cedar Bar (now under Diablo Lake), then crossed back to the north side and went over Sourdough Mountain to a point north of Ruby Creek, where still another bridge brought a packer or hiker to the Slate Creek/Ruby Creek diggings.

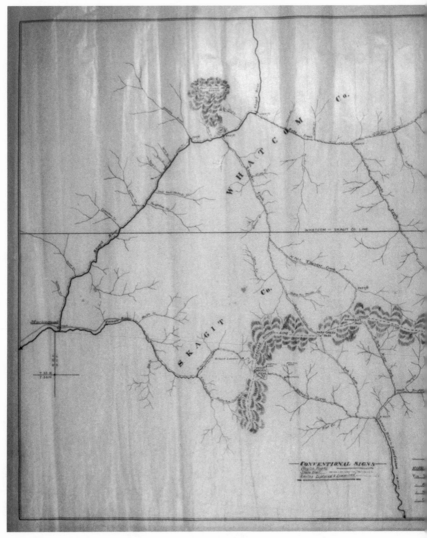

1893 State Road Commission map created for construction of the Cascade Pass road of 1896-97. (Photo courtesy of BBIC map collection at the Center for Pacific Northwest Studies, Western Washington University, Bellingham, Washington).

The Cascade Wagon Road Fiasco

The State Road Commission, with a flair for gracious understatement, commended the local people and said that the trail was "picturesque and shows the energy displayed by the active interests of the Slate Creek mining district in opening of ingress and egress." But

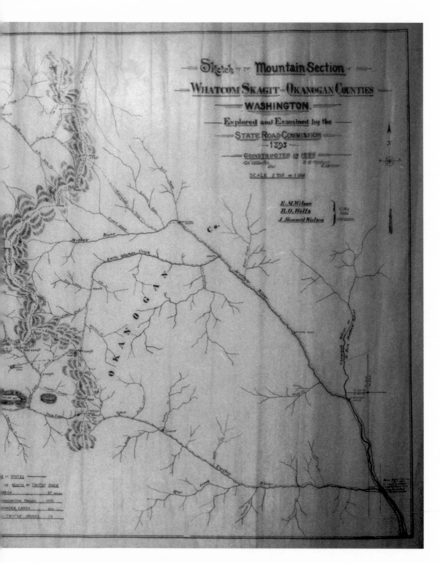

after their surveyors spent an exhausting two months in the mountains, the State discarded the gorge as passable only for horses (even that marginal) and decided to build along the old Indian trail of Red Fox over Cascade Pass.

Considerable work ensued on both sides in 1896. The eastsiders continued to work on the portion approaching Cascade Pass, proceeding over Twisp Pass to the Stehekin River and Bridge Creek. M. E. Field, who ran Field's Hotel at Stehekin (the site now under water), contracted

53

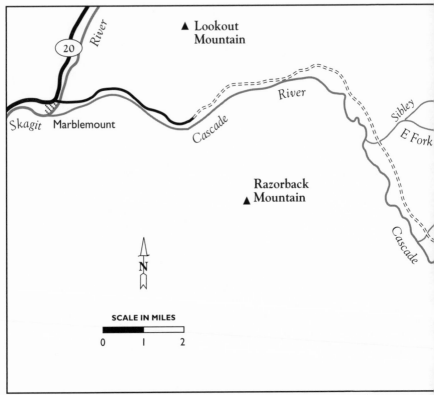

Route of the Cascade Pass road, the first recognized trail through the North Cascades.

to construct bunkhouses for crews and supply them. A road crew mem-ber earned $2 to $2.50 per day, from which 75 cents per day was deducted for room and board. On the west side work crews improved the Cascade River road to Lookout Mountain, about six miles above Marblemount, at which point large boulders obstructed the path. Workmen bridged from one narrow ledge to the next, managing to construct another six miles of road to Gilbert Landre's cabin, about three miles from Cascade Pass.

The Road Commission's meager funding necessitated scrimping on costs. The Commission's report stated:

the work had to be done without a survey except at the most critical parts of the route, and only four feet of the road bed could be graded where heavy excavation was necessary. But the Board, recognizing the necessity of the thoroughfare, made brush and timber cuts from sixteen to twenty feet in width and removed rock and stumps from the roadway; thus making practically a wagon road width except on rock barriers and steep side hills.

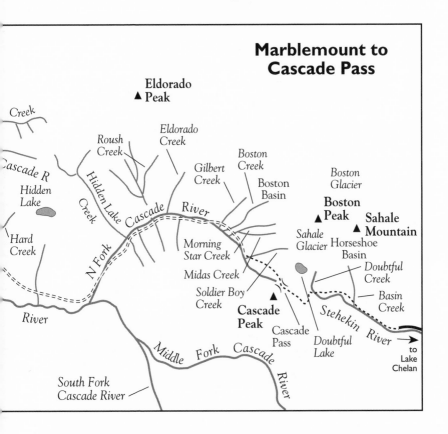

Marblemount to Cascade Pass

Those "excepts" and "practically" were misleading. Work was incomplete on both sides of Cascade Pass. Only a pack trail existed from Landre's cabin over the pass to the eastsiders' termination point somewhere near the "Stairway," the extremely steep southeastern face of Cascade Pass. No wagon ever went over the trail. This did not deter the media from declaring that the road was now fit for a team and wagon. The *Chelan Leader* reported in 1897 that "An Olympia dispatch says the Cascade division of the state wagon road from Marcus to Marblemount is completed, leaving $7,400 of the $20,000 appropriated . . . to finish up the road in Stevens County [over the pass]."

Before 1897 was over storms took out most of the new work along the Cascade River, while eastsiders continued to repair damage caused by severe flooding in 1894. The flood also destroyed parts of the Methow–Barron road (Hart's Pass). In 1899 the State repaired some of the Methow bridges and built twelve and one-half additional miles of narrow road toward Lake Chelan from Bridge Creek, stopping three miles short of the lake. To demonstrate how good the road was, Methow miner George Rouse rode horseback fifty-three miles from Twisp to the Cascade Pass summit in one day plus a few hours, half the previous travel time. However, that was one man and a horse, not a wagon. In 1905, Joseph M. Snow, the first appointed State Highway Commissioner, went to see the road personally and declared that almost all the money invested had been a total waste. In 1911 State Representative Bowlby recommended that the Cascade Wagon Road be abandoned, too. He said the appropriated funds were not spent and the route was impractical. Also the proposed route would go through the new forest reserve, making it difficult to obtain rights-of-way. The Cascade Pass wagon road, despite media hype, never existed at all. It was then and still is a rugged trail.

Route Variations

Because of renewed mining interest early in the twentieth century, a bill was introduced in the State Legislature on January 27, 1905, proposing that $25,000 be spent on a road from Marblemount to a point near Mill Creek in the Slate Creek area. On March 9, House Substitute Bill No. 25 passed without opposition, appropriating $24,000 for survey, construction, and maintenance of such a wagon road, plus the improvement of the Methow–Barron road. Whatcom County would contribute $8,000 and Skagit County $5,000 toward the effort, and the two counties did some work on the trail, not yet a wagon road.

The effort collapsed in a political fracas between the two counties. For some time Skagit County had stalled in building a connecting road to Bellingham with funds received from a sale of rights-of-way to the Great Northern plus matching funds from the state. Because Skagit refused to allocate such matching funds, fearing competition from Bellingham in the supply business, Whatcom County refused to work on the wagon road.

In 1905, the state legislature created the position of State Highway Commissioner and gave him guidelines for a new state highway system. One of Commissioner Joseph M. Snow's first actions was to offer Skagit County $5,500 to add to their Great Northern funds to build the road. Skagit County commissioners rejected the offer on the basis that the route along Chuckanut Bay was impractical, that they were considering a road via Samish Lake. While the counties were at a stalemate, angered miners proposed forming a new county out of parts of eastern Whatcom and Skagit. On September 1, 1905, the state government asked for a Writ of Mandamus against Skagit, Snohomish, and Whatcom

County commissioners to force them to proceed with the Bellingham road. The Bellingham Good Roads committee of the Chamber of Commerce sided with the state in urging the construction.

C. N. Adams of Bellingham made a new survey, but still no new road resulted. On March 9 when matters still were at a stand-off, Commissioner Snow sued Skagit County to force it to build to Bellingham, but Skagit won in court. In 1907 the state legislature amended its road policies so that counties were no longer required to match state funds for road building *but* if a county requested help for any state roads within its borders, it had to ask. Skagit did not ask. In 1909 the state began building the Chuckanut Bay road (today's Chuckanut Drive) with convict labor, but it was not completed until 1920 due to politicking and World War I. By that time the poor Slate Creek miners had given up hope and, besides, the mines were not productive, so the Mill Creek–Slate road never was built.

In 1903, W. A. C. Rowse had proposed building an electric railway from Skagit to Horseshoe Basin in Cascade Pass to serve the miners, but that proposal died. During 1907, under the leadership of eastside Senator W. A. Bolinger, the State Good Roads Association was organized, a group of dedicated volunteers. The state legislature designated the non-existent road from Marblemount to Barron as state road 11 and the nonexistent Cascade Pass road as 13; state road 12 from Pateros to Robinson Creek was completed in December 1909.

The old miners' trail from Hart's Pass to Newhalem was still in use by horsemen and hikers. In an article for the Bellingham *American-Reveille*, September 1, 1907, "Old Flint" wrote about a pleasure trip George D. Pierce, W. F. Roehl, and he took, guided by Bart Edwards of Wenatchee. He told of the excellent hunting around Early Winters Creek, and of encounters down valley with huge rattlesnakes. (He wrote that local settlers had a superstition that a man never missed a rattler, that the snake attracts the bullet, invariably getting in the line of fire.) The account mentions the mostly abandoned settlement of Robinson Creek:

> A hotel, a few houses and a barn is all there is of the settlement. A lot of mining machinery awaits transportation to the mines above. And all along the route are fragments of machinery, as if the teamsters, tiring of the titanic job of lifting it thousands of feet into the mountains, had dumped it along the wayside, disgusted and discouraged with the task.

"Old Flint" said that at 4,000 feet on August 18 ice covered the water pail in the morning at a mail carrier's cabin called The Layout, a few miles east of the Hart's Pass summit, where the party spent the night.

On the descent from Hart's Pass into Mill Creek they found mining camps but continued the following day toward the Davis farm in Skagit Canyon—a twelve-hour ride. The writer commented:

> Over Sour Dough and along the Goat Trail the horses had been beset by yellow jackets. In their fright and fury they would sometimes bolt, but they passed the worst places safely, and we considered ourselves fortunate the animals were not stung where the trail would permit of no sidestepping.

The party eventually arrived at Bellingham after covering 250 miles in the saddle. Other than packers who supplied the Slate and Mill Creek prospectors, that trail was little used.

Citizen Groups

Despite the problems with the North Cascades, Governor Marion E. Hay declared a "Good Roads Day" in 1912. In January of that year, the Skagit Good Roads Association was organized. It included E. W. Ferris, Pat Halloran, John Finstad, Alfred Polson, J. O. Rudene, John Meehan, Charles Nelson, W. H. Franklin, Ed Barben, M. P. Hurd, P. W. Trueman, W. S. Stevens, S. S. Gay, and G. B. Grace. At first the organization pushed for improvement of a north–south road, ignoring the North Cascades, since the counties were at a stalemate over that project anyway. On January 14, 1913, the legislature passed a bill providing for a levy of $1.5 million and subsequent levies of $1 million annually for state highway use, delineating the projects.

Renewed interest in a North Cascades road came from the media. In 1916, the famous author, Mary Roberts Rinehart, wrote of her horseback trip over Cascade Pass for *Collier's Magazine*. Rinehart found the trail perilous. In her autobiography, *My Story*, she wrote that the sixteen members of the party included her husband, two boys, and Bob Mills of the Great Northern Railway. Following are excerpts from her account:

> To get all of us across a sloping ice field with a drop of a half mile below was arduous and nerve-wracking. And again and again we found ourselves in dangerous places, with no choice but to go on. To my own weariness began to be added anxiety for the other members of the family. A slip, by horse or man or boy, and there would be inevitable tragedy. For never had I dreamed of such a country; it was beautiful, but rugged and wild beyond belief. There were abysses appalling to the mind.
>
> [*Author's note:* I believe the following must have been at the eastern wall of Cascade Pass.] We held a conference that night. Across that barrier . . . was safety for ourselves, food for the horses. True, it meant climb-

ing to a lake up a tortuous cliff, and after that and without a trail, scaling another eight hundred feet of mountain wall . . . Mr. Hilligoss . . . , small axe in hand he cleared a way; he threw down rocks, he blazed a route on any scrub he could find. . . . For the climb up that cliff the next day I have no words. . . . How we got down the wall I do not remember. It took long hours of switching back and forth, with again Mr. Hilligoss on foot, testing ledges, examining slopes. We made it at last, but our troubles were far from being over. Also our nerves were gone. Beyond the pass was one frightful spot where it was necessary to go through a waterfall on a narrow ledge slippery with moss, from which the water dropped a thousand feet without a break into the valley below.

[Little feed for the horses was found.] It was on a morning near the end that Doctor Rinehart fed his horse a biscuit, an apple, two lumps of sugar and a raw egg. And the horse ate them all.

Despite the designation on paper of state roads 11 and 12 as the "Roosevelt Highway," State Highway Department engineer Charles I. Signer denounced that nonexistent road and endorsed Cascade Pass, a fixation that persisted until the U.S. Forest Service and Seattle City Light required access through the Skagit Gorge.

Around 1920, Skagit and Okanogan County businessmen formed the Cascade Pass Pilgrims to promote the Cascade Pass highway. Among the initial leaders were David McIntyre, David Donnelly, Albert Mosier, Charles Gable, Burt Moody, Tom Chambers, and Allan Moore. Eastsiders Senator W. A. Bolinger, Harry J. Kerr, Leonard Therriault, L. D. "Les" Holloway, Irwin Stokes, and others joined their westside friends in lobbying for the road. The members had memorably enjoyable times in the process. They scheduled dinners, luncheons, and barbecues, and collared columnists, news writers, and legislators in an effort to interest the public in fighting for a cross-mountain highway. David McIntyre and a Sedro-Woolley surveyor, Albert Mosier, made a survey of the pass on their own, and Pilgrims lobbied the Good Roads Association groups.

The Pilgrims staged imaginative promotions, annual events for the members starting in 1926, and individual promotional trips on horseback for legislators or the media to see (and write or talk about) the magnificence of the North Cascades and the need for access by the general public. In 1928 both east and west contingents trekked to a meeting place at Cascade Pass to have a barbecue and make speeches. The Pilgrims included a big delegation from the Spokane Chamber of Commerce, supporters from Grant, Okanogan, Douglas, and Chelan (the

Four-County Council), and a Great Northern Railway representative cognizant of the tourist potential of a road. Here were some of the opinions expressed:

The Cascade Pass highway is the one possible chance to build a highway that would successfully compete with the Columbia River highway and keep people within the state of Washington after they reach the Spokane gateway.

—E. F. Banker, state legislator

The people of the east side are behind the pass to a man. Eastern Washington needs good roads and we must help them to get a clean, oiled road through to Spokane, before we could get full benefit of the Cascade Pass highway.

—E. U. Springer, Mount Vernon photographer

The scenic beauty of the Cascade Pass highway is unexcelled . . . peaks crowned with perpetual snow, waterfalls and beautiful little lakes.

—Dr. Alfred Hendricksen, Burlington

There was even one comment about the cook:

No matter what happened . . . and it was raining pitchforks when we got to the summit [in the prior year], before you could eat your mush the bowl was half full of rainwater and the hotcakes were swimming . . . Orville [Widden of Marblemount] never once lost his smile.

—Fred Graham, Seattle Rotarian

The formalities dispatched, the entire contingent hiked to Stehekin, boarded a barge down the lake to Chelan for a banquet, then traveled to Twisp for a rip-snorting rodeo in honor of its guests.

The next year's pilgrimage was also an adventure. The eastsiders hired a barge tied between two boats to take them from Chelan to Stehekin. An orchestra played, the sun shone warmly, laughter and jokes were the norm. After a couple of hours the barge began to sink and was beached at Safety Harbor. Passengers treated the whole interruption as a lark. Many ate picnic lunches, others went swimming, and the band played on until the craft was repaired. The party arrived at Stehekin by dinnertime. The next day all forty-eight people began the hike to Marblemount to witness the dedication of the new Marblemount bridge and to hear speakers Governor Roland Hartley and Samuel Hume, State Director of Highways. Among the Pilgrims were reporters from the *Seattle Times* and *Wenatchee World*. The difficulties of the trip made good copy.

In 1924, Governor Roland Hartley had influenced the state legislature to appropriate $70,000 for the Marblemount–Cascade Pass section, and another $150,000 in 1927 plus $35,000 more for a bridge across the Skagit River at Marblemount. The Skagit commissioners pledged labor and equipment in lieu of cash matching funds.

In 1929, though, the additional $200,000 appropriation expected from the state legislature did not materialize—the stock market crashed, and during the depressed 1930s no one had money for anything. In a memorable meeting in 1940 of the Regional Forest Service officials in Portland, road boosters led by Pilgrim L. D. Holloway joined with Forest Service and State Highway Department personnel in scrapping forever the Cascade Pass route. One contributing factor was interest in the Skagit Gorge, where by 1925 Seattle City Light had built Gorge Dam, after constructing a supply road into the canyon. Another factor was the focus of the USFS in constructing fire-fighting trails into the Cascades.

Because of World War II pressures nothing further was done about the matter until 1953. To illustrate the abysmal condition of even the existing upper Skagit Valley road, a Seattle City Light employee said that, during heavy rains in 1947, the graveled road around Diobsud Creek turned into mud holes so deep that one did not dare get out of the car. Also, the road was barely wide enough for two vehicles to pass. On Rockport Hill it wound through the trees, and farther east, on Talc Mine Hill and Shovel Spur, winter snows and ice made driving treacherous.

Ten Years of Lobbying Gets Results:
The North Cascades Highway Association

Despite the apparent disinterest on the part of state government in a cross-mountain road, legislators did approve appropriations for mine-to-market roads, which affected the approaches to the North Cascades from both sides. None crossed.

In 1953, highway boosters held a meeting in Okanogan to organize the North Cross-State Highway Association (known after April 18, 1971, as the North Cascades Highway Association). Widespread citizen interest resulted in representation from Island, Whatcom, Skagit, Chelan, Okanogan, and Ferry Counties, who raised a loud, irate common voice that it was not fair that there were five cross-mountain highways in the southern 60 percent of the state, and the northern 40 percent had none. The new Association elected officers, planned to have two annual meetings (one on each side of the mountains), and started work on a promotional campaign aimed at both the public and government representatives. Political pressure was definitely to be used to get action.

The new president of the Association, Sig Berglund of Sedro-Woolley, issued invitations to key legislators, the governor of Washington, and other officials to come to a road-planning meeting at Sedro-Woolley. Absolutely no one responded. Thoroughly angered, Berglund sent a telegram to each stating crisply, "Meeting cancelled due to lack of interest on the part of State officials." His telephone rang incessantly as politically embarrassed officials apologized.

Most attended a rescheduled meeting, where the Association members presented a logical plan for a cross-mountain road. Elected officials could not ignore the power of the members of the well-organized group—a majority agreed to support the effort. The Association promised not to interfere with the details of route and construction, and would try to gain public support for appropriations. The thrust was to tout the highway as a recreational road and an access to valuable timberlands since, by now, commercial vehicles were using Snoqualmie and Stevens Passes. The tourism planners envisioned the highway stretching from Okanogan through the mountains and Whidbey Island to the Olympic Peninsula (with a necessary ferry to Port Townsend). The optimism of Association members sank when they learned in December 1954 that $25 million was to be allocated for roads in Skagit and Whatcom Counties, but none for a cross-mountain highway.

While road boosters sat gloomily contemplating the future that fateful night, Bill Bugge, State Highway Director, suddenly exclaimed, "Say, do you know how you might get this thing off the ground? Maybe the federal government would be willing to appropriate some funds for new forest access roads." So began political and private pressure on timber companies and the Bureau of Public Roads to create such roads. Whether coincidental or not, two months later on February 24, 1955, U.S. Forest Ranger Frank Lewis of Marblemount told the Upper Skagit Booster Club that he had received a request for a huge timber sale in the Granite Creek area, conveniently located between Diablo Lake and the crest of the Cascades along the route recommended for a cross-mountain highway.

This proposal fell through, but in October 1956 Al Frizzell of the U.S. Engineers began surveying for a bridge across the Skagit River above Gorge Dam and admitted that the Mount Baker National Forest was considering a road to Thunder Creek. Losing no time in capitalizing on the breakthrough, the 1957 Association president, Les Holloway of Twisp, and a committee met with the State Highway Commission. The result was that the state and the U.S. Bureau of Public Roads agreed to build the road to Thunder Creek to state standards so that it could become a segment of the cross-mountain highway.

In July 1957 State Engineers Fred Walter and Walter Theiss entered the Cascades from the east (the Early Winters area) on reconnaissance for a connecting route beyond Thunder Creek. They were accompanied by a packer employed by Jack Wilson, a professional guide and North Cross-State Highway Association enthusiast. About this same time the Association scheduled the first of its flashy promotional trips for politicians and influential people who could encourage the flow of appropriations for the highway. These trips continued until the highway opened in 1972. Experienced horsemen such as Sig Hjaltalin, Les Holloway, George Zahn, Jack Wilson, and others over the years accompanied people like legislator Morris Bolinger, Mayor Wade Troutman of Bridgeport, and District Engineer Paul McKay. The trips were arduous but sported excellent camp cooking, fun, scenery, and captive audiences for the Association boosters.

On September 12, 1957, while engineer Ike Munson was locating a route from the east (a detailed, step-by-step road survey), the Association brought a delegation from the east to meet others from the west at Ross Lake, including writer E. P. Chalcraft of the *Seattle Post-Intelligencer*, whose feature story and photos were timed to appear just before the Washington Good Roads Association convention in Longview. Although successful from a promotional standpoint, the trip was otherwise a nightmare. Horses were assembled from several sources and, strangers all, they squabbled and fought all night, facing each new day crabby and unsettled. George Zahn's own horse bucked him off, and on another day reared over backwards. Zahn took it all in stride, commenting only that he swallowed half his cigar. The yellow jacket season was on, and a beautiful Arabian horse sustained 190 stings that almost killed him. Frantic horses kicked or bolted. Cameras and objects tied onto saddles flapped around to further frighten the mounts. Fortunately, no one was hurt seriously, and reporters bravely wrote about the beauties of the Cascades.

After his survey, engineer Munson threw his influence behind the North Cross-State Highway Association, talking with influential federal and state highway engineers and planners about the road. After the convention at Longview the Good Roads Association added its endorsement. Things seemed to be going well. In 1958, with Bellingham's Sig Hjaltalin at the head of the Association, a new roadblock arose—the possibility of declaring the entire area from Ross Lake to the Methow Valley a national wilderness area. Julia Butler Hanson, head of the Roads and Bridges Committee, asserted there was no public interest in the highway, whereupon the Association collected a caravan of ninety cars bearing 200 people from all over Washington state to parade from

Members of the North Cascades Highway Association trekked across the mountains on horseback to survey possible routes.

Everett to Olympia to show support. Media coverage helped the cause. Hjaltalin and State Senator Fred Martin then chided USFS officials with cutting and stacking logs indefinitely along the proposed truck road to Thunder Creek. Hjaltalin spoke approvingly about judicious timber harvesting:

> I have seen great cedar logs downed, some as much as six and eight feet in diameter lying down. It will just lay and rot and be a terrific fire hazard, a bug-breeding place. Anyway, who likes to see a burned-over area. Who likes to look at a ragged stump up high with a tree hanging limp from it, part of it lying on the ground, so rotten one cannot even sit on it for a picnic.

At first Seattle City Light fought the road, preferring its splendid isolation in the Skagit Gorge to opening the area to the public, even though it had discontinued its rail service to the dam sites. Major supplies came by tug and barge on Ross Lake. Their opposition was lukewarm, however, and the Association eventually gained their support. Everything seemed in place for a speedy completion of a cross-mountain highway. Ike Munson predicted that, if the state and federal governments would appropriate the money all in one lump, the highway could be completed for an estimated $11 million. It was not to be; too many other choruses of wants faced each state legislature. By the time the highway was finished piecemeal in 1972, it had cost $23 million.

Opposition from Conservation Groups

The marriage of loggers and highway builders did not proceed without resistance. On August 2, 1960, the Sierra Club voiced its opposition to activities in previously uncommitted national forest lands, stating in *The Sierra Club Bulletin*:

> The Sierra Club knows that logging is entirely necessary on most of our forest land, perhaps ninety per cent of it. But on part of the remaining ten per cent, it believes that preservation programs should receive major emphasis. When the forest service, in planning activities such as these three [the Thunder Creek proposal plus two unrelated ones in California], makes it clear that it does not intend to expand its wilderness dedications to meet the needs of today and the future, it becomes obvious why [when] so many conservationists have decided to get the wilderness preservation job done, they just turn to another agency, the National Park Service.

This was to be the alignment of many preservationists for ensuing years, even as the U.S. Forest Service was in the process of forming new wilderness areas (such as Glacier Peak) in addition to the already existing 801,000-acre North Cascades Primitive Area. Richard E. McArdle, chief of the U.S. Forest Service, was quoted in a 1961 *National Geographic Magazine* article:

> Various groups have criticized our wilderness policy. But we assess National Forest land—its timber and other resources against its value as wilderness—before making a decision. At Glacier Peak we've established a wilderness area where it is most valuable as wilderness.

Some within the North Cascades Highway booster groups staged a protest march against the formation of the Glacier Peak Wilderness Area during the summer of 1960. Horsemen from both sides of the mountain met at Miner's Ridge near Glacier Peak. This was a media event, for the North Cross-State Highway Association already had sent formal resolutions to government agencies protesting locking up more forest lands. Despite the unified resistance to Glacier Peak Wilderness by a majority of the counties involved—Whatcom, Skagit, Okanogan, and Chelan— it was created on September 15, 1960, by Ezra T. Benson, Secretary of Agriculture. Opponents asserted that the lack of logs created by the two new wilderness areas caused the layoff of an entire shift of millworkers at the Wagner Mill in Twisp.

Meanwhile, the preservationists through the North Cascades Conservation Council of Seattle enlisted the help of Congressman Tom Pelly toward obtaining North Cascades National Park. Pelly asked the support of the Secretary of Agriculture and requested a moratorium on further logging of the area and on further appropriations. Congressman Jack Westland differed with Pelly and felt that, with the two vast wilderness areas already approved, a national park was unnecessary and that controlled timber cutting should continue because of an acute log shortage. In April 1963 the Council asked for a park of 1.3 million acres, and Secretary of the Interior Morris Udall and Agriculture Secretary Orville Freeman authorized a North Cascades Study Team to investigate the best use of the area from Mount Rainier to the Canadian border. Frank Brockman stated in *American Forests* magazine, September 1966:

> This Act [establishing the National Park Service, August 25, 1916] stated that the purpose of the NPS was to promote and regulate the use of the Federal areas known as national parks, monuments and reservations . . . to conserve the scenery and the natural and historic objects and the wildlife therein and to provide for the enjoyment of the same in such manner and by such means as will leave them unimpaired for the enjoyment of future generations. The NPS proposal for this park was predicated upon extensive development for large numbers of people with ready access by road, trail, water and air, including an aerial tram [and] involves concepts not in accord with national park philosophy.

At a June 1966 meeting of the Washington chapter of the Wilderness Society in Wenatchee, Patrick Goldsworthy, president of the North Cascades Conservation Council, called for enlarging the boundaries of the proposed park. He pointed out that the Olympic National Park had been created in the face of diverse opinions from state agencies, Game Department, local communities, and the USFS, but that local chambers of commerce admitted later that the park expanded local economies. President Lyndon B. Johnson and Senator Henry Jackson were in favor of a park but did not specify areas.

The National Park Service and the U.S. Forest Service continued to battle over jurisdiction. In August 1966 Orville Freeman came to look at the area, reiterating his position that he saw no reason to duplicate administrative organizations within the area, managed for over sixty years by the USFS.

In March 1967 the Department of the Interior submitted to Congress a proposal to establish the national park, plus a new national recreation area, a national forest wilderness, two extensions to existing wilderness area (Ross Lake and the Pasayten), and the extension of the Glacier Peak Wilderness to include parts of the Suiattle River and White Chuck River corridors. In April hearings on the matter began in Washington, D.C., with heated opinions voiced by groups for and against the park and wilderness areas, and with varying specifics as to the acreages. Supporters of the bill included Washington State Governor Dan Evans, the Conservation Council, Senator Brock Evans, and Outdoors Clubs of eight western states. Opposing were representatives of industrial forestry and the director of the Washington State Department of Game (primarily because of proposed prohibitions against hunting, which he claimed maintained strong herds of wildlife).

As the hearings moved to Seattle and Wenatchee, support came from the Sierra Club and Washington Alpine Club, American Alpine Club of New York City, The Mountaineers, and others, with opposition from Pacific Northwest Ski Association, the Seattle Chamber of Commerce, Washington State Cattlemen's Association, North Central Washington Sportsmen's Council, and Seattle Sports Fishing Club.

On November 2, 1967, after listening to all sides, the U.S. Senate passed the bill establishing the North Cascades National Park, totaling 1.2 million acres. President Lyndon B. Johnson signed the bill October 2, 1968. The Forest Service lost jurisdiction over 301,000 acres of government lands to the National Park Service. A corridor to accommodate the North Cascades Highway was set aside in the bill.

Several proposals fell through. Among them were the building of a tramway at either Ruby Mountain or Colonial Glacier and others at Arctic Creek west of Ross Lake and at Price Lake; a ferry across Ross Lake from Rowland Point to Hozomeen (with a stop at Arctic Creek); and several hostels. There simply was no more money to be found for such improvements.

The North Cross-State Highway Association might have opposed the park but, when the bill had been passed, influential member David McIntyre commented, "The North Cascades Park is here. . . . For those of us who might have questioned the idea in the beginning, it behooves us to work now for its full development." The momentum of the highway effort was too great to stop easily. In June 1962, Governor Albert Rosellini indicated approval of the highway at the annual meeting of the Association at Concrete. Other attendees were Elmer C. Huntley, chairman of the House Roads Committee; Nat Washington, chairman of the Interim Senate Committee on Highways; George Zahn, newly appointed and key booster in the State Highway Commission; Ernest Cowell, chairman of that commission; Bill Mason, Bureau of Public

Roads engineer; three state senators and a brace of state representatives. Most were then behind the completion of the highway. During the last years of the 1960s a powerful team of legislators and senators, including Warren Magnuson, Henry Jackson, Tom Foley, and Lloyd Meeds united to request Federal Public Lands Act funds and various other available appropriations from the U.S. government. After his election in 1966, Governor Dan Evans continued support for the highway. To monitor the proposed routing of the final segments of road, Governor Evans rode horseback in late August 1966 from Silver Star Highway camp (between Early Winters and Washington Pass) to Ross Lake. He was accompanied by Emmit Aston of Omak; Clare Pentz, then president of the Association; Bruce Wilson of the *Omak Chronicle*; two free-lance writers; and Evans' son Danny. Aston said everyone fell in love with the little boy and said he was a good scout even when his mount, an old gray mare, plunged through deep holes in fording Granite Creek.

A portion of the Skagit River was designated as a Wild and Scenic River in 1968. Completion of the North Cascades Highway was not affected, but both opponents and proponents agreed that the builders and users should be controlled as to destruction of natural scenery and the integrity of the river systems.

The outcry of preservationists helped to make the North Cascades Highway more beautiful. The appearance of the Highway was designed by a committee consisting of representatives of the Forest Service, State Highway Commission, Federal Bureau of Public Roads, a landscape architect, and others. As retired Forest Ranger Harold Chriswell stated in 1972, previous highways were carved straight through the forest like a tunnel. Instead, the North Cascades Highway builders sloped the banks gently, selectively cut trees so travelers could see up and away from the road toward the peaks, and planted grass. The latter invited wild animals to graze and the open areas blossomed forth with wildflowers.

The Road Builders

As indicated earlier, the North Cascades Highway was assembled piecemeal. In the 1920s the road from Pateros on the Columbia River to Winthrop and Mazama became passable. In August 1927 the Federal Bureau of Public Roads allocated $60,000 for improvement of the Loup Loup forest road, now a segment of the North Cascades Highway from Twisp to Okanogan. On the west side a road existed to Newhalem, primarily to supply Seattle City Light's dams. A section between Newhalem and Thunder Creek resulted from timber harvesting. By February 1960 a temporary bridge crossed the Skagit River below Diablo—not without problems, for the swift flowing river actually bent the derrick drilling pilings. At the east end of the route a crew worked near Early Winters to extend the road from Mazama toward Washington Pass.

On Labor Day, 1960, the North Cross-State Highway Association staged a publicity stunt to show how the completed roads already were speeding cross-mountain travel. Methow Valley residents challenged Skagit Valley citizens to a horseback race across the highway route. Jerry Sullivan represented Methow, and Oscar Peterson rode for Skagit. Horses were stationed every eight or ten miles on the trail, and riders were to change horses, but one of Sullivan's mounts escaped and he rode the same animal for two segments. Peterson covered the entire route with his own two Arabians, alternately riding one and leading the other. Despite the logistics problems, Sullivan won by about an hour.

In 1961, Okanogan County was declared a distressed area. This sparked the Twisp Chamber of Commerce, Jack Abrams of the Association, and the Okanogan County Commission to inquire if the highway could be built with Federal Distressed Area funds and alleviate unemployment. That same year George Zahn was appointed to the State Highway Commission, putting him in a position to influence allocations of highway funds. Governor Albert Rosellini voiced his support, and the State Highway Department's director Bill Bugge verified that financing seemed assured, with the west side receiving funds from the Federal Bureau of Public Roads, the east from the state of Washington.

Construction commenced in earnest. Goodfellow Brothers of Wenatchee gained the major contract for clearing the roadway on the east. Mac Lloyd of Twisp was a subcontractor for clearing, while Jack Wilson installed and moved camps and packed supplies. The first camp was near Indian Creek about six miles above the mouth of Early Winters Creek, the second at Willow Creek, then Cutthroat, and so on. Displaced rattlesnakes were a menace to workers. Horses frightened by noisy equipment bucked off their riders. From Cutthroat Creek to Washington and Rainy Passes advance crews fought through solid rock. Concerned about scenic preservation, they modified the dynamite charges so that nearby trees would remain standing. Crews hauled out rubble to distant locations as fill.

A few men brought their families to live in tents at the camps. At Lone Fir three families roughed it. The men worked six days a week and long hours, especially since the working season at the high altitudes was short. Their families amused themselves by watching the myriad wildlife, making pets out of magpies, rabbits, deer, or simply keeping track of their youngsters. Baths were a problem, since the creeks were glacier runoffs, but the chilly water and snowbanks that lasted far into the summer did act as natural refrigeration.

Whistler Mountain on the western slope of Washington Pass (Photo by JoAnn Roe).

Crews tackling the west side and Skagit Gorge had lower altitudes but encountered dangerous conditions while disturbing the unstable rocky cliffs. The ticklish job of widening the road from Newhalem to

Diablo was awarded to Canadian firms: Highway Construction, Ltd., and Emil Anderson Construction Company of Richmond, B.C. Accidents were inevitable. In October 1962 Jack Turner of Clear Lake (Skagit Valley) was buried by fifty tons of rock as he worked his 'dozer. A week later Glenn Stafford of Concrete was buried by a major slide as he sat in the cab of his tractor. A lookout was posted while machinery worked in the Gorge; if so much as a boulder fell, he sounded an alarm. Even so, Alfred Clark of Marblemount was lost in April 1963 while scaling rock in a location thought to be safe.

Nonetheless, work continued and Senator Henry Jackson stated on May 15, 1964, that only thirty miles separated the two crews.

Seven avalanches hit the Gorge that next winter, bringing snow-slides as deep as 12 feet and as long as 150 feet, which had to be cleared away before construction could proceed. Chuck Wolf, who worked for both Goodfellow and Wilder during construction, said that the terrain was alternately solid rock and talus. The rock could be blasted and the talus gave way readily to earth-movers, but the latter was unstable and hazardous. The hillsides between Diablo Lake and Ross Dam were little better, because chasms and runoff from several waterfalls had to be bridged. Horsetail Falls (later renamed John Pierce Falls) was two waterfalls separated by a narrow ledge that tilted toward the Skagit below. A crew under Wolf prepared, sanded, and graveled the ledge to accommodate heavy equipment. During the initial preparation in 1965, the brakes failed on a large shovel and it plummeted into the canyon. The operator jumped to safety. Pieces of the shovel are still there in the underbrush. Drivers of the first off-highway trucks slated to cross the ledge refused, until shamed by Wolf's driving the first truck himself. No wonder their hearts were in their mouths: the ledge was so narrow that one of the truck's rear dual wheels hung over empty space.

A curious problem with the waterfalls during spring and fall was that enormous, dangerously heavy icicles would form nightly. Someone had to knock them down before trucks and crews could work.

One morning a slide buried bulldozers and equipment at No-name Creek, two miles east of Horsetail, so thoroughly that only a 'dozer's exhaust pipe marked the burial spot. To protect their workers from slides, contractors installed screens around the operators' cages on earth-moving equipment. Despite the danger, the operators considered the job a challenge and most continued working.

By 1968, only a few places required more work but one posed a for-midable problem—how to bridge the chasm, 200 feet deep, at Horse-tail (Pierce) Falls. K. K. Larsen of Seattle gained the contract for the 335-foot steel span. It was impossible to get to the bottom to pour

Old horse trail bridge across one of the many streams rushing into Granite Creek (Photo by JoAnn Roe).

concrete piers for the bridge, so Larsen's crew rigged a cable across the canyon, from which all materials—including wet concrete—were suspended and lowered to create the piers. A heavy crane at one end of the cable handled placement. To protect against falls, a net was stretched across the canyon. Workmen swung in boatswain's chairs from the cliffs to set great steel anchors for the supports.

When all was ready, girders weighing eighteen tons, each 110 feet long in a single piece, 10 feet deep, were hauled one at a time up the narrow road from Newhalem. In places the road had to be reinforced to support the extreme weight. Once on site, one end of a girder was fastened to the high cable and drawn carefully across the canyon, where the other end was eased into place. Once the girders were in place, the bridge was finished quickly. In accordance with environmental standards, Larsen darkened the bridge's concrete to match nearby rocks.

Nature was not finished with the highway crews. One July day they sweltered in 80 degree temperatures but awakened the following morning to 15 degrees and eighteen inches of snow on the ground.

Finally a crude pioneer road existed all the way, and in September 1968, four-wheel-drive vehicles, dune buggies, motorcycles, horses, and one passenger car (driven by the author's husband) made the trip to Rainy Pass for a major celebration of the North Cross-State Highway Association and highway supporters. As eastsiders and westsiders met, symbolically one vehicle with Les Holloway of Twisp sitting on its hood and a second with John Pierce of Bellingham crawled slowly toward each other until the two could clasp hands. A crowd of about 2,000 in 400–500 vehicles roared their approval.

It was a politician's field day; anyone who could claim some part in the planning or funding of the highway came. Senator Warren Magnuson dropped in by helicopter; Representatives Tom Foley and Lloyd Meeds, the state senators, and mayors were there. Ken King, then president of the Association, introduced Governor Evans for a speech and a pitch for reelection. Charles Prahl, State Director of Highways, added his comments. In a carnival atmosphere on a warm fall day, the crowd devoured chili and hamburgers provided by the Winthrop Kiwanis Club.

Then the finishing and paving crews went to work. James Parkhill was project engineer for the State Highway Department between 1968 and 1973; Wilder Construction, Associated Sand & Gravel, and Materne Bros. were responsible for most of the paving. Two major bridges were still in process—the 563-foot Baker River Bridge at Concrete, and the Panther Creek Bridge east of Horsetail Falls. On Rucker Brothers trucks the six giant girders for the Panther, each 130 feet long and weighing 98,000 pounds, brushed the cliffs while rounding curves on a narrow detour road that bypassed Lillian Creek.

During the winter of 1971–72 a slide came down near Whistler Mountain between Washington and Rainy Passes and wiped out the crew's cabin, destroying everything. On the west, Wilder Company crews prepared the road for paving and departed for the winter. In March

A crew works to rough out part of the North Cascades Highway, about 1971 (Photo by JoAnn Roe).

Chuck Wolf of Wilder and Tom Simpson of the Bureau of Public Roads bumped over the roadbed from Thunder Arm to get ready for spring, only to find that a huge slide about three miles west of Granite Creek had crossed the creek and dammed it to form a large lake. The slide lay about fifty feet deep on the roadbed—perhaps 250,000 yards of rubble to remove—and Wilder faced a projected September 1972 opening.

It took twenty men and several big Euclid trucks just to remove the slide. Water continued to run through the debris, making conditions unstable. Two operators quit in concern for their safety. The crew first shaved off rock and dirt from the lower side of the slide, thinning the barrier until it was only ten to fifteen feet thick. Then a bold bulldozer operator made a decisive pass at the remainder, sweeping halfway across and swiftly backing out. Water boiled through the opening, washing away much of the remaining debris. Because Granite Creek is a spawning stream, the crew carefully reconstructed the creek bed, spacing out some rocks for fish havens and removing others. Their remodeling job won them a letter of commendation from the Fish and Game Department.

The pressure of completion before September began to get to the crews. Wolf told the author that one day a big, tough man sat in his office and cried—just from stress. To relieve tension, Wilder threw a big weekend party for the men and their families. The change of pace helped. Paving crews, although hampered by the loss of a crane over a cliff, worked up to the very morning of the September 2 opening date. Figuratively, at least, the asphalt was still smoking when the caravan of cars streamed over the highway. The Wilder Company sent a very stressed Chuck Wolf on a vacation to Hawaii.

Opening of the North Cascades Highway

Opening Day dawned bright and clear on both sides of the mountain. Three dedications of the highway ensued, starting at Winthrop, followed by Newhalem, then—as dusk began to fall—at Sedro-Woolley's high school ball field.

At Winthrop honor guards of smartly attired horsemen fittingly moved among the large crowd in the old western town. Leonard Therriault, East Side President of the renamed North Cascades Highway Association, gave welcoming remarks. Master of Ceremonies was Hu Blonk, managing editor of the *Wenatchee World*. The colors were presented by the Tumwater Area Council Boy Scout Troop 101, and the Winthrop School band played the national anthem. Special guests made short speeches, including Governor Dan Evans, Congressmen Thomas S. Foley and Mike McCormack, Federal Highway Representatives Lewis Lybecker and Pat Clark, National Parks Representative Lowell White, National Forest Representative Gerhart Nelson, state legislators Joe Haussler, William Schumaker, and Bruce Wilson, West

Side Association President Ernest Johnson, and Department of Highways Commissioner Harold Walsh and Director George Andrews. Governor Evans presented special plaques to Douglas and Bruce Zahn and eight pioneer boosters of the highway. With forty-niner Queen Linda Collins looking on, the ribbon was cut and a caravan formed to travel to the next dedication.

Ex-governor Daniel Evans speaking at Opening Day of the North Cascades Highway, Winthrop, September 2, 1972 (Photo by JoAnn Roe).

At Newhalem Ernest Johnson was Master of Ceremonies. Presentation of colors was by the Concrete Cub Scouts, followed by the Concrete High School band playing the national anthem, and an invocation. Special guests at this ceremony were Seattle City Light representatives, including Skagit Project Manager Thomas Bucknell; Mayor Wes Uhlman of Seattle; Congressman Lloyd Meeds; presidential representatives; and representatives of all the agencies honored at the Winthrop ceremony. Governor Evans addressed the crowd from the back of a pickup truck and later participated in a second ribbon-cutting to open the next segment of the highway.

At Sedro-Woolley most of the same dignitaries were present, as well as Edward Nixon, brother of President Richard Nixon, who addressed the crowd as an official presidential representative. A detailed historical presentation and slide show about the highway was available, as well as refreshments for the famished group that had thrice dedicated it.

The next day a river of cars streamed over the completed road, even though it still needed turnouts, lines, and signs. One hundred fifty-eight years had passed since Alexander Ross first searched for a cross-mountain road. The effort began with commerce in mind but ended in opening a wonderfully scenic highway. The beauties of the North Cascades are now open to all—rich, poor, hikers, handicapped—from March until heavy snowfalls force closure of the highway sometime around November.

[*Author's note:* A list of contractors involved in building the highway (1959–72) is given in the Acknowledgments.]

6. THE SETTLEMENTS

The Methow Valley

Winthrop (believed to be named for Theodore Winthrop, author of *Canoe and Saddle*) was founded by storekeeper Guy Waring in 1891, consisting of only a few buildings. Native people had occupied the site at the junction of the Methow and Chewuch Rivers for generations, gathering camas bulbs, catching and drying fish, and pasturing their horse herds on the valley's lush grasslands, as related in Chapter 2. A presettlement epidemic of smallpox or measles apparently wiped out most early natives, because the first Europeans in the valley found skeletons and bones all along the Methow River, scattered in a manner that suggested rampant deaths and flight from contamination. Yet summer residents returned to customary sites until the mid-twentieth century.

The Methow Valley was designated part of the Chief Moses Reservation in 1879, but Moses sold it back to the U.S. government in 1884, and the valley was opened to homesteading in 1886. About this time brothers Tom and Jim Robinson set up a hunting camp at today's Winthrop, but they soon moved on. James Sullivan, Walter Frisbee, and several other families settled near the site about 1887–88.

Near today's Sun Mountain Lodge and Patterson Lake, John Pleasant Rader and George Rader claimed lands in 1888, moving to the valley in May 1889. Three other families lived there by fall 1888: Rans

Moore, Jewitt Davis, and Harvey Nickell. Before Waring came to Winthrop, other pioneers included the Pearrygin, Boesel, Filer, and Thompson families, as well as Charles Look (who founded the Winthrop post office in June 1891). Conditions for those earliest pioneers were described by Laura (Mrs. Fred) Thompson in a 1914 *Methow Valley Journal* reminiscence:

> [Upon arriving at the cabin her husband had built earlier in the Wolf Creek area] Proudly he led me into the 14-by-16-foot cabin with a dirt floor. It was gloomy and damp inside. . . . I sobbed and nearly collapsed into his arms. . . . The valley had been lovely—but it had been blackened by a big fire . . . at least I could fix up the cabin. It contained a mission-style table, two crude benches, a pole bedstead, a grindstone, a keg of white beans, a plow, and a saddle hung across a center beam. . . . But several crates had been shipped with me, and I set to work. Soon we had the dirt floor packed solid and smooth with nice clean water. As each crate was emptied, we broke it into slats and laid them as walkways inside the cabin. . . . Sometimes I'd get so lonesome and scared . . . I'd climb on the cabin roof and scream. . . . In April, eight months after I had arrived in the Methow, I got my first mail—12 letters.

Laura Thompson was the first to encounter the Warings as they came into the valley.

Guy Waring, a Harvard graduate, left his father's engineering business in Boston to seek his fortune in the West, first landing at Loomis, Washington, to open a store with Julius Allen Loomis. The business folded and, after a brief return to Boston, Waring traveled to Winthrop's site with his wife and three stepchildren. The Warings suffered through a harsh autumn in a tent, moving in November to an adequate, if basic, log cabin. Waring's store opened for business in January 1892 with $2,100 worth of merchandise purchased on credit. The log cabin was said to be below freezing all winter because it had no door—only a blanketed entry. Since the nearest supply point was at Coulee City, a hundred miles distant, settlers still were grateful for the new store.

During 1892 budding author Owen Wister, a Harvard friend, came to visit Waring and enjoy goat hunting. He returned in 1898 and spent part of his honeymoon on a horseback trip over War Creek Pass to Lake Chelan with his bride, Waring's wife, daughter, a guide, and a cook. Certain characters and situations in his book *The Virginian* are believed to be patterned after Methow Valley people and experiences.

Waring endured notably bad luck. During the winter of 1892–93 his dwelling burned, forcing the family into a cramped sixteen-by-twenty-foot cabin. During that unusually harsh winter, the snow was so deep that horses could not uncover grass; some survived by chewing pine branches and each other's tails. One Okanogan homesteader fed his horses boiled potatoes.

Waring left for Michigan to earn money to refinance his Methow operations, hiring local homesteader Walter Frisbee to operate the store. Frisbee enjoyed a different philosophy of business operations from Waring. In a letter to Waring, August 7, 1893, Frisbee wrote:

> The great fault with mee is that I care nothing at all for money for its own Sake and I often times loose sight of the advantages which money brings and Rate them as of no consequence. Now this is all wronge according to the Standard that the world works up to. . . . I have entered into this business with a view to making a success of it and if through any missmanagement on my part it should be a failier. Remember that I will stand between you and eny *actual loss*.

Later in his letter Frisbee added: "You will perhaps notice a slight difference in Mr. Websters Spelling compared with mine. This I am convinced was not Mr. Websters fault."

Waring's relations with Frisbee were intolerable—one stern, the other apparently easy-going—so he next hired Earl F. Johnson to manage the store after entering strict terms of management. Business still was slow, partly because of the 1893 economic depression, and Johnson conceived the idea of building a social hall and holding dances at the "Forks" (Winthrop) to attract business. The dances, literary society meetings, and amateur theatricals did help, but were insufficient to create much profit. In December 1896 Waring returned to Winthrop and managed to hang on financially. He organized the Methow Trading Company to exploit the possibilities for economic gain during the mining boom in Hart's Pass and other nearby sites. Seventeen investors (including Waring, his stepson Robert Greene, and Earl Johnson) incorporated with an initial capital investment of $17,500, raised through the sale of capital stock. All except the westerners were from Boston. Seventy-five hundred dollars was to be used to acquire Waring's existing store, water rights, and land; the balance was for additions and improvements to the holdings, including a grist mill, portable steam sawmill, cattle, hay, buildings, a hotel, and a feed station. At this time, Waring owned every building in Winthrop except the town hall. He built a spacious new log home the locals soon dubbed "The Castle" on the bluff above town. He installed comfortable furniture, 350 volumes of classics, and his wife's Mason Hamlin organ.

Going briskly to work, Waring wooed shoppers by building a cable ferry across the river and, although he deplored liquor, he opened the

Duck Brand Saloon—named for an old Harvard University students' hangout—to forestall potential competition. The saloon was sternly regulated. The bartender was not allowed to talk to patrons except to take their orders. Patrons were watched closely for signs of inebriation, and the saloon closed early. Waring's unorthodox and unpopular rules were offset by the provision of quality liquor and tobacco—no rotgut concoctions. He soon had competition when David Heckendorn platted his own town south of Waring's site in 1904, adding a store operated by Chauncey R. "Dick" McLean.

The apparent success of the mines prompted Waring to open a branch store at Barron and, as settlers flocked into the Methow in growing numbers, others at Pateros and Twisp, and a small post at Robinson Creek. Supplies came to Winthrop from Pateros by packhorse and later by wagon. To meet the growing need for mining timbers and homes the Methow Trading Company built a sawmill along the Methow River seven miles north of Winthrop. Land was a profitable commodity, and Waring planted an orchard in 1904 on holdings he called "Land 5" between the forks of the Chewuch River. It proved to be a financially disastrous move, absorbing profits from other ventures. The orchard was totally destroyed by unusually dry weather and lack of irrigation in 1915.

Meantime, another Methow pioneer, Leonard Therriault, came to work at Waring's store in 1910–11. After gaining further business experience at a Twisp store, Leonard and his brother Paul opened a freighting business in 1915 between Pateros and Winthrop. On a typical day the teamster left Winthrop with milk cans, perhaps live chickens or hogs, a bit of gold, maybe a passenger or two, then stopped for the night at Gold Creek and resumed the journey to Pateros the next day. The return trip to Winthrop took another two days, and sometimes more when horses and wagons became mired in mud. As roads improved, freight and mail moved by Model T Ford. In winter the freighters switched to horse-drawn sleighs or a Therriault invention—a Model T cut down to sled width so the hard tires could operate in the packed-down sled tracks of the roads. The prospering Therriaults later purchased Waring's store in Winthrop.

Waring's optimistic appeals for stockholders seemed warranted. By 1916 the $17,500 investment had grown to $168,914, but well over half was in land, so cash flow was tight. Waring's supply businesses waned with the decline in mining, and the Robinson and Barron stores closed by 1905. The stores at Twisp and Pateros closed in 1910, as did the Duck Brand Saloon, after Waring and the bartender were arrested for operating the business without a license—an unfounded claim arising from confusion about when to pay the fee. Contributing to Waring's business problems were competitive stores and apparent resentment of Waring for (1) asking to have the town's post office changed to the name "War-ing" and (2) refusing to allow his neighbors to build an irrigation ditch across his land, while he had already obtained a water rights claim for a substantial amount of water from the Chewuch River. At the end of 1916, with another operating loss, the investors removed Waring from control of the company.

Poor Guy Waring gave up and moved back east in 1917, although he returned in April to be entertained at a Winthrop reception for his new bride (his first wife had died in 1906). For the next fifteen years the Methow Trading Company's investors attempted to liquidate the operations profitably, but by 1931, the company no longer operated, and its corporate license was allowed to lapse for nonpayment of fees.

Eyeing the verdant timber stands on the surrounding foothills, men opened sawmills in the Methow Valley, including the Ballard, Fender, McKnight, and Wetzel Mills, plus a longer-lasting operation owned by Otto Wagner at Twisp. Simon W. Shafer started a meat market at Winthrop in 1922, subsequently expanding his business to include gro-ceries—in the face of intense antagonism from the two existing mar-kets. Shafer hung on and endeared himself to the poverty-stricken settlers during the Depression by bartering for antiques and artifacts or extending credit. So great did his collection of memorabilia become that he was forced to find a new location to house it. He acquired Guy Waring's old "Castle" in 1943, used by the Episcopal Church since 1922, and Shafer's collections formed the nucleus of the Shafer Museum in August 1976.

The town was platted in 1897 by the Methow Trading Company, and the plat of sixty-nine lots was approved on January 11, 1901, by the Okanogan Board of Commissioners. Winthrop had telephone service (the lines ran on interconnected barbed wire fences) and a newspaper, *The Winthrop Eagle*, by 1909, the Farmers State Bank in 1912, and er-ratic electric lighting by the early 1920s. In the early 1900s Hubert Flagg opened the Forks Hotel, successively known as the Dodd Hotel, Winthrop Hotel, and Winthrop Palace.

A stage service from Pateros was operated by E. R. Davis (driven by his brother "Preacher" Davis) and later by Ray Calvert. In 1907 the Methow Trading Company had a store and Tom Wills another. In addition to the Duck Brand Saloon was one operated by Charlie Graves. Two creameries thrived eventually, the Bluebell and the Okanogan. A Mr. Haase led a local band. The Heckendorn Opera House encouraged locals to use their acting talents. In 1916 Harry Green built a hotel and stage stop on the present site of Three-Fingered Jack's.

Dr. E. P. Murdock opened Methow Valley Hospital around 1924, only to watch it burn in 1927.

With such amenities, several stores, and a U.S. Forest Service ranger station established in 1917, the town was incorporated in 1924. R. E. Johnson was the first mayor and R. W. Flourney the city clerk. At least two English families settled at Winthrop, Lt. Aldridge and Hugh Frazier. Frazier was a former English ambassador to Japan and a general in the Boer War. Why persons of such background came to settle in remote Winthrop was a closely held secret.

The sport of rodeo began casually in Winthrop. After a ball game one man would challenge anyone to ride his bucking horse. Soon there was a contest for best rider, with betting and prizes. In Okanogan County a Native American, C. B. Susan, created a big canvas-walled arena, then staged rodeos with horses and riders, but no bulldogging or roping. Later professional rodeo developed, with stock contractors like Okanogan's Leo Moomaw furnishing the bucking horses.

The upper Methow had its tribulations. The winter of 1915–16 all but isolated Winthrop with a smothering total snowfall of thirteen feet eight and one-half inches for the season. A full one-third of that fell on February 10. The average settled-down snowpack was more than four feet on the flat. That spring the melting snow filled the Methow River to flood stage, the highest in fifteen years, taking out bridges and undermining banks. The rampage was repeated in 1933 and 1948, both

A sign in the center of Winthrop tells of the founding of the town (Photo by JoAnn Roe).

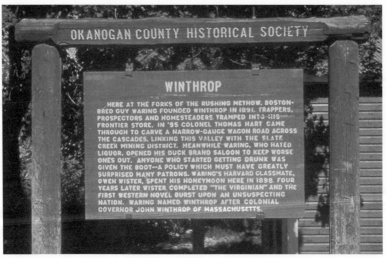

times destroying the big bridge at the south end of Winthrop. The 1933 destruction of the bridge was initiated by adverse frequencies set in motion by a herd of cattle being driven across it. During the 1948 flood, water was six feet up on the walls of riverside homes. Since the Methow River has a considerable current, huge waves crested in the middle. Waters were said to move with the speed of a locomotive. When flood-waters reached the Winthrop fish hatchery, 310,000 blueback salmon fry escaped a bit earlier than intended. The Heckendorn section was hard hit. Entire rows of homes were washed away and disintegrated. Leonard Therriault's mother, Mrs. Nick Peters, returned home to find water lapping at the hems of dresses hanging in her closet. Elinore Drake remembered the 1948 destruction, saying: "We watched a big tree come down and slam into the pilings of the bridge and, when it went down, I'm afraid all we kids had to say was, whoopee, we won't have to go to school for awhile [the school was on the opposite side of the river from Winthrop]." The reprieve was short-lived because the citizens rigged up a cable car for passenger traffic across the river, and school soon resumed.

Crime, seldom seen in Winthrop, reared its ugly head October 18, 1926. Thieves first broke into the Kenison Furniture Store and stole four mattresses to muffle the explosion, then blasted open the outer door of the Farmers State Bank vault during the night. The interior of the vault was littered with debris, but the internal strongbox, which was on a time lock, was intact. All the robbers gained was $600 in silver and currency not yet placed in the strongbox, plus three $50 Liberty bonds. They were never caught.

Fires burned Murdock's hospital and Nickell's store and creamery in 1927. Another fire in 1929 consumed Therriault's store.

Inspired, perhaps, by the writings of travelers such as Mary Roberts Rinehart, who regularly visited the famed Eaton's Ranch in Wyoming, Methow Valley people conceived the idea of opening resorts to take advantage of the sunny weather, spectacular scenery, and horse-oriented lifestyle. North of Winthrop on the Chewuch, Paul Spaeth opened the Methow Valley Dude Ranch in the 1940s. Much earlier, at the turn of the century LeRoy Wright founded Pearrygin Lake Resort on the spring-fed lake indenting the bench above Winthrop. Hunters willing to dispense with luxuries rented the two rough cabins. Two resorts—Derry at the site of Wright's original resort and Silverline nearby—and a neat state park near Pearrygin's original homestead provided camping facilities in the late 1900s on Pearrygin Lake. The lake is fed by Pearrygin Creek and a spring, covering about 320 surface acres. Considered a "production lake," Pearrygin hosts 80,000–90,000 rainbow fingerlings planted each year, a bonanza for fishermen who pull in grown trout twelve to fourteen inches long, some weighing five pounds. The lake came under the management of the Chewuch Canal Company in 1921 to serve as a reservoir.

In the 1930s Dr. O. J. Blende purchased the Sunny M Ranch, a working cattle ranch at "Crazy Corners" homesteaded by Clint Shulenberger and later operated by state representative E. F. Banker. The ranch lands extended as far as Patterson Lake and beyond Thompson Ridge. Blende converted the ranch to cater to dudes and sold it to Manson Backus as a combination cattle and dude ranch, the guest quarters consisting of rooms in the original, spacious ranch house plus eight cabins. Under the management of local horseman Foss Creveling, the ranch prospered. Every Sunday the Sunny M hosted a local rodeo, using rancher Ray Thompson's horses. According to Sally Portman in her book *The Smiling Country*:

> "Wild" cattle were supplied by any animals that got lost and wandered out of their own range onto Sunny M land. Under the pretext of bringing them to the Sunny M to alert their owner, the boys would just "borrow" the heifers for rodeo riding. "After all," chuckled Archie [Archie Eiffert, a wrangler], "wouldn't want to burn calories off our own cows!"

Joe Barron, descendant of a Methow Valley family and relative of Alex Barron, founder of the Barron mine, owned and operated the ranch from 1950 to 1965. At first he retained the main house and cabins, adding a swimming pool. Later he moved the cabins to the Patterson Lake Resort. Barron acquired exotic birds and set them free on the ranch. Quality horses served both dudes and family for trail rides. The Barrons simply had fun with the Sunny M. According to a private history of the ranch written by Mark Barron and quoted in Portman's book:

> Everyone looked forward to the family-style meals served at the ranch house which were always lively and fun. Often, someone played the piano and stirred up a real cowboy atmosphere. My dad had learned to be a superb meat cook while living on an Iowa farm, so every Sunday night he cooked a huge standing rib roast which he proudly carved for the guests.

Around 1965, Joe turned over the management of the Sunny M to his son Jack, a Seattle businessman. Jack quietly acquired 4,000 acres of adjacent property. The Methow Valley was named a depressed area, which helped Barron obtain financing and approval of resort development plans from the Economic Development Administration. By then environmental protection had become an issue; the Barrons had to get

Patterson Lake near Sun Mountain Lodge, Winthrop area (Photo by JoAnn Roe).

forty-one permits over a three-year period. Certainly the Barrons' interest in birds helped. Jack raised ducks and geese to liberate on Patterson Lake and left snags in trees to provide nesting sites for eagles.

The successor to Sunny M, Sun Mountain Lodge, opened in May 1968 with a main lodge, two units of guest rooms, swimming pools, hot tub, tennis courts, a restaurant, convention facilities, horses for trail rides, and all the amenities of a luxury guest ranch on a site high above the valley with sweeping views of the North Cascades Mountains.

Twenty-one years later the operation was purchased by Erivan and Helga Haub. Erivan Haub was a supermarket magnate and owner of Tengelmann Group, Germany. The Haubs had gotten familiar with the valley during several pack trips with upper Methow packer Jack Wilson. They also purchased the splendid home built around 1950 by Otto and Kathryn Wagner on the Chewuch River north of Winthrop. The showplace, still standing, was designed by Robert Jorgenson and partially built by Jack Wilson. It has six windowed sides to admit mountain views, an octagonal barn, a pond, and elegant landscaping.

In 1972 Kathryn Wagner, then widowed, stepped in to encourage and partly finance the "invention" of Winthrop (until then a typical small farming town) as a Western town with boardwalks and frontier ambience. Small-scale farming was declining and the town languished as better roads and faster cars made it possible to shop in the larger towns of Omak, Wenatchee, or Spokane. A deep freeze in 1968 destroyed many of the orchards, and in 1971 the Winthrop Auditorium collapsed under the weight of a heavy snowfall. A new era was dawning, though, as the North Cascades Highway seemed likely to be completed. The road would pass right down the main street of sleepy Winthrop.

Requesting the help of architect Robert Jorgenson, Kathryn Wagner presented plans for a new/old Winthrop to the merchants and Kiwanis Club. She said if each merchant would contribute $2,000, she would donate the balance needed to complete the project. Enthusiastic merchants complied and the funds were held by the Kiwanis Foundation for disbursal. Wagner and Jorgenson researched old western towns and architecture. False fronts for buildings, paint that made exteriors look weather-beaten, and board sidewalks to cover perfectly good concrete ones soon transformed twenty buildings on the main street. Artist Chet Andrizzi and a crew painted the sides of some buildings with advertisements of old products such as Bull Durham tobacco.

Opening day of the North Cascades Highway came all too soon. A breathless merchant cadre braced for the onslaught of tourism. It was as overwhelming as expected. The capacity of restaurants and the few lodgings were taxed beyond belief in the little town of four hundred residents. One weekend near the end of the 1973 season, a restaurant's supplies were so depleted that it offered only two items on the menu, and the fully booked Trail's End Motel personnel called as far as Chelan to find accommodations for stranded travelers. The proprietor even lent people blankets and pillows to sleep in their cars.

During the following years townspeople managed to build, plan, and execute facilities to care adequately for the tourists. They even encouraged more by staging bluegrass music festivals, rodeos, a forty-niner

Downtown Winthrop in 1972 after it was transformed from a typical small farming village to a Western town with boardwalks and frontier ambience (Photo by JoAnn Roe).

festival, an antique car rally, and such. Fire destroyed the original corner landmark, the Winthrop Emporium, and another store in 1993, and the historic Winthrop Methodist Church burned in 1994. The Emporium was rebuilt as a replica of the original and opened July 29, 1994.

Hart's Pass

Barron was located off the Hart's Pass Road and is discussed in Chapter 4. Only traces of the first and second Barron towns remain at the present time.

Ventura was located a short distance from today's Yellowjacket Sno-Park east of the Lost River Resort on the Hart's Pass Road. During gold rush days it consisted of a few cabins, tents, and shelters for supplies being transported to the high country mines.

Robinson was a larger but short-lived settlement that thrived at the turn of the century at Robinson Creek and the Hart's Pass Road. The town may have sprawled across both sides of the creek. It was large enough that Guy Waring established a branch store to supply the miners, but he closed the operation in 1905 when gold fever subsided. At the request of Waring, Mazama's postmistress Minnie M. Tingley prepared an application for a Robinson post office on October 28, 1900, giving the population as "10 in winter and 50 in summer." After the post office was established on December 15, 1900, the two postmasters were R. E. McDonald and James S. Owens, but the service was discontinued December 31, 1902.

Lost River Resort was adjacent to the site of Robinson. Hazard and Zora Ballard made their home at Lost River, and the present-day Lost River Airport Association property is his original 160-acre homestead. The water supply for the property owners is from Ballard's original artesian spring near Ventura. One blue spruce tree (not native to that site) and a bearing apple tree planted by Hazard Ballard still survive at the site. The Lost River Resort includes a 3,200-foot dirt airstrip serving private aircraft owners.

In the late 1950s a restaurant at the site, operated by "Swede" Logan and Robert Hadway, boasted such fine cuisine that customers came from miles around to dine and swim in the outdoor pool. Hadway also flew his Stinson Gullwing on USFS reconnaissance. Pete Arnold purchased the property from Hadway and proceeded to develop lots on the Lost River airstrip. Jim Sandon acquired Lost River Resort from George Moate in the late 1980s. The resort presently consists of cabins but no longer has an operating restaurant. The name "Lost River" is believed to stem from the fact that the river goes underground for a time and emerges as an arm of the Methow River.

Mazama, never more than a crossroads settlement, was small but important as the junction of the Methow Valley county road and the Hart's Pass Road. It was originally located a bit southeast of its present site, and was called Goat Creek, but when the U.S. Post Office Department did not accept either Goat Creek or Goat Mountain as a name,

Looking west/northwest into the upper Methow Valley, where a road crew labors in the distance to complete the North Cascades Highway (Photo by JoAnn Roe).

Guy Waring suggested the name "Mazama," Spanish or Indian for a Rocky Mountain goat. The first post office was established June 1, 1900, with Minnie M. Tingley its first postmistress. The site was a jumping-off place for the Slate Creek/Hart's Pass mines—a beginning point for the supply trains and for winter dogsled trips of pioneers like Ed Kikendall. Probably it had a supply store at the beginning of the century, and a store still operates 100 years later. The mail came to Tingley's home. Twice a week the trip was made over muddy roads or deep snows, by horse, wagon, sleigh, or car as time progressed. When road conditions deteriorated, local farmers used horse teams to drag logs along and smooth the roads so the mail could get through. Tingley bound the incoming mail into bundles, so that anyone arriving under adverse conditions, perhaps by snowshoe, could drop off mail to neighbors on the way home, and it was said she kept a pot of hot soup to fortify the patrons.

Around 1918 Angus O. McLeod operated an inn about a half mile from Mazama and later ran the store, restaurant, and post office at Mazama's present site. In the late 1950s Andy and Gladys Russell also had a store in the same area.

Contact with the outside world was little better by mid-century than it had been in 1900. An article in the October 1, 1959, *Wenatchee World* tells the story of Dorothea Albin, then the mail carrier from Winthrop to Mazama and beyond:

> Every weekday morning after 8:00 A.M. you'll find her somewhere along the route, clad in Levis, a corduroy jacket, and a happy grin. When she reaches Mazama, she [goes] as far as Lost River (her Tuesday–Thursday–Saturday route). No one lives the year round beyond that point due to the tremendous Hart's Pass snows. She has only four boxes to fill out of Mazama in seven miles on one side of the river, and only seven boxes in five miles on the other side.

Albin was supposed to be back in Winthrop by 5:30 but tended to serve as the big sister to all the residents. The *Wenatchee World* article continued:

> People ask her to pay their light bill in Winthrop or pick up some groceries for them, or haul back some feed next day, or they hook a ride to Winthrop. About two or three times a week she goes to the Winthrop school, either to deliver kids who missed the bus, or to take lunches and books they overlooked.

Among the early residents were Ellis and Martha Peters, Walter and Nella Foster, Graden Patterson, and William and Vi Pederson (Bill owned the store, Vi was the postmistress in the 1940s). On today's site of the Mazama Inn and The Ranch House, a rancher named Kagle filed a homestead claim and raised cattle. He was followed by Allen Stookey, who built the block-walled dwelling now called The Ranch House inn. Wally Eggleston purchased the ranch in 1959, raised about a hundred head of beef cattle, and sold the property to Harold Bowers in 1976.

Bowers's wife Glenna worked for the Pasayten Ranger Station at Early Winters and later for the Twisp Smokejumper Base. At this time other ranches near Mazama included the Callaway & Castle Ranch, Foster and Patterson farms, and a ranch owned by Don and Dorothy Shafer.

Snowfall around Mazama was legendary, averaging four feet of snow-pack. Wally Eggleston maintains that seven feet of snow fell one Easter day, so light that a saddle horse could walk beneath the surface of the snow and only his rider's head and shoulders were visible above. Eggleston operated a U.S. Weather Service station at the ranch, recording each day's snow level, moisture content, and temperature—a frigid -52 degrees one day in the late 1960s. He said the nearby sawmill ran all week just cutting pieces of wood to feed the boilers.

The awesome crags of the Goat Wall at Mazama are riddled by mineral exploration holes. Mount Flagg has more than 100 such holes. According to recent Mazama store operator Steve Milka, a mine was developed in the 1920s by Alvie Sharp near Mazama. About five miles up the Hart's Pass Road toward Robinson Creek the Mazama Queen Mine operated in the 1970s. Harold Bowers's mother cooked for the mine crew. After the mine ceased operations, the cookhouse was moved to Bowers's ranch and used as a chicken coop. During the time Bowers owned the ranch, a miner named McCain worked the American Flag Mine adjacent to his property, bringing ore by cable and buckets down to a bin at the foot of the mountain. The cable broke one day and killed two men.

Mazama's chief importance over the years was simply its location as the last possible place to buy supplies or gasoline before tackling the Hart's Pass Road or other upper valley and mountain locations. The store has changed hands several times, most recently operated by Jeff and Dora Sandine.

In 1980, Cal Merriman, Eric Sanford, and George Mayercak purchased Bowers's ranch property. They expanded the original ranch house to serve guests, and opened "The Ranch House" as an inn to serve the patrons of Liberty Bell Alpine Tours, for which Sanford was the helicopter operator. The group offered heli-skiing, mountain climbing, survival tours, and cross-country skiing. Around 1983 the three men built the handsome Mazama Inn, a lodge and restaurant, which later was acquired by Cal Merriman and his wife Ann. Added to the list of activities was horseback trail riding under the auspices of Aaron Burkhart, Jr., of Early Winters Outfitters.

Cross-country skiing as a sport mushroomed to the extent that in 1996 Tom Kimbrell built a new sporting goods store at Mazama to rent skis, mountain bikes, and so on. The Mazama Inn was sold in

Matchless autumn scenery delighted travelers who crossed the old Methow River bridge between Winthrop and Mazama (Photo by JoAnn Roe).

1994 to Bill Pope and George Turner, and The Ranch House (plus horse facilities) was sold to Steve Devin.

Devin remodeled The Ranch House to a smart Western theme, offering patrons the convenience of stabling their private horses there. Non-horse owners could arrange trail rides with Winthrop packer Claude Miller. Devin and his father Doug also operated a cow/calf ranch nearby.

Meantime, across the North Cascades Highway from Mazama, Jack and Elsie Wilson operated the Wilson Ranch, renting cabins and offering pack trips into the North Cascades for several decades (see Chapter 8).

In the late 1960s entrepreneur Doug Devin worked with Wilson and others to attempt development of a major downhill ski operation on Wilson's property and adjacent lands. For twenty years a pitched battle raged between those for and against the proposal, which included the building of condominiums and major resort facilities (see Chapter 8). The project was finally abandoned.

In 1992, R. D. Merrill Company of Seattle acquired the land and joined with Lowe Development Corporation to form the Methow Valley Limited Liability Corporation, present owners. The seventy-four acre Wilson Ranch portion of a planned destination resort called Arrowleaf was approved and the Freestone Inn was ready for occupancy in 1996. The log inn, located near Jack Wilson's former home, has twelve rooms all equipped with native-stone fireplaces, a fine restaurant, a pond, and careful plantings. The inn continues to expound the Wilson mystique of hospitality, enjoyment of natural beauty, and mountain trips. Management refurbished Wilson's old cabins, retaining the rustic appearance but increasing their comforts. In August 1996 the company finally obtained permits to develop the rest of the 1,200-acre resort, with a golf course, tennis courts, horse operation, and up to 600 homes to be built over a twenty-five- to thirty-year period. Where the Aspen-style proposal had failed—downhill skiing and much larger in scope—the smaller Arrowleaf project with cross-country skiing has been more widely accepted. Aspects of the development are still being contested, however.

Along the Skagit

Newhalem, on the western edge of the North Cascades, originally was called Goodell's Landing and was located at the head of navigation for the Skagit River, about one-quarter mile downriver from today's settlement. N. E. Goodell set up a trading post in 1879 at the site to serve miners, as did "Amsey" Clothier and E. G. English in 1880. At one time Gorge pioneer Lucinda Davis operated the store.

When Goodell came into the Skagit, he became fast friends with the two chiefs of the Upper Skagit Indians, John Campbell and John Quwoitkin. Goodell claimed to be a key figure in resolving a dangerous confrontation between the native people and U.S. troops around 1880 (see Chapter 2). He wrote that Quwoitkin sent for him to attend a tense meeting to decide whether to confer with a government representative or go to war, and that his (Goodell's) speech at that meeting swayed them to talk, not fight.

Within a few years Goodell sold his store to Henry Dennis, who in turn sold the business and land to a German immigrant, August Dohne. Dohne rebuilt a two-and-one-half-story building following a disastrous fire. In 1898 the upper Skagit was included in the Washington Forest Reserve, although the 1906 Forest Homestead Act permitted homesteads to be granted if the claimant had lived on the property at least five years and if no significant amount of valuable timber was included. Dohne applied for title to his property (on which he had cleared ten acres, plowed three, and planted fruit trees). At the time the Skagit Power Company was eyeing the same area as a potential power project. According to Paul Pitzer in *Building the Skagit,* Charles Park, the forest supervisor, militantly opposed private ownership in the forest and went to great lengths to deny Dohne rights to his land, conjuring up numerous accusations to support the position. Each barrier was proven to be false and Dohne finally won title in 1910—possibly because the Skagit Power Company had decided to build elsewhere. In 1913 his roadhouse burned but was rebuilt. Dohne became seriously ill in 1918 and died. His property was eventually sold to Seattle City Light.

Another resident's title was denied. Burton Babcock, schoolmate and occasional traveling partner of author Hamlin Garland, purchased his land and lived on it intermittently from 1892–97, but often was away prospecting or working. He went with Garland to the Yukon gold rush, returning in 1904. Despite Garland's appeals to Gifford Pinchot on behalf of his friend, Babcock's homestead claim was denied because he had not lived on his land for five continuous years prior to 1906.

The settlement of Newhalem was born of tents, later replaced with cabins after Seattle City Light started its dams. Almost 500 men came to live there with their families, a public school opened with joint financing by Seattle City Light and the county, and other amenities followed. A popular roving minister who had worked in the logging camps, Rev. L. H. Peterson ("Parson Pete") came in April 1921 from the Bellingham Presbytery. He organized not only church services but also well-attended social events and published a newsy little paper called *Fits and Starts*. Population swelled to 1,000 and citizens argued about the town's name—Goodell's or Newhalem. College students hired to work for the summer settled the issue forever. In the early 1920s, just prior to the arrival of a group of Seattle officials, the students hung a big plank sign at the entrance to camp, saying "Welcome to Newhalem." The name is derived from *ne-whalem*, an Indian word meaning "goat trap."

Seattle City Light built new homes for the workers as soon as practicable—a neat, planned community with lawns, playgrounds, and tennis courts. The "Hillbilly Hotel" was the bunkhouse for foremen (across from Skagit Store), later leased to the National Park Service for an information center. Jack Ferrar managed the building for some years, before moving to the company's Seattle office.

Newhalem received telephone service in 1948. Installation of a microwave communications system in 1954 solved the problems of downed lines during bad weather. A meeting hall housed community functions but it burned in 1958 and was replaced by an auditorium named Currier Hall after Dana Currier, the first Skagit Project supervisor. The first doctor in Newhalem was Donald R. Crow, followed by Dr. Fritz.

In earlier days children boarded out during the high school year, either at Sedro-Woolley, Mount Vernon, or Seattle. After the high school at Concrete opened, the children went to school by train until Seattle City Light removed the railroad in 1954, then by bus, thirty-two miles each way. Even so, until the advent of the North Cascades Highway there was only a one-lane, wooden bridge over Goodell and Bacon Creeks, built in 1933–34 by the Civilian Conservation Corps.

Veteran City Light employee Ed Scott came to Newhalem for a three-month temporary job as a maintenance carpenter and wound up staying thirty-four years. Scott's daughter Dolores married Victor Hundahl, who succeeded Dana Currier as supervisor of the Skagit Project (retiring in 1964), and in 1994, their son Donald, a self-styled "third-generation Skagit Brat," was appointed supervisor after working up through company ranks.

The supervisor was not one to sit in an office. In 1948, a major slide blocked the railroad between Rockport and Newhalem. Snow lay six to eight feet deep on the flat, and no trains ran for six weeks. Supplies were brought in by tracked vehicle and sled. At the Gorge Dam Archie Jones and two other employees stayed on site to keep the intake gates free of debris. They began to run short of food. Victor Hundahl and twenty men using Coleman lanterns and handcarts took groceries and acetylene torches to Jones' crew through the two-mile twenty-two-foot diameter diversion tunnel.

The supervisor of the Skagit Project automatically becomes the "mayor" of both Diablo and Newhalem. His office manages both company towns where most employees are on "key" status, receiving free housing and free utilities. Only five outsiders were on "renter" status in 1996: an employee of the National Park Service, the bus driver, the deputy sheriff, and two others. Renters have to pay for housing and utilities. Seattle City Light is responsible for supporting the needs of the communities with a plumber, sewage treatment, landscape maintenance, carpenters, painters, and such.

Newhalem and Diablo always enjoyed a brisk social life that assuaged the loneliness of the residents. Gale force winter winds often howled through the Gorge and snows easily could paralyze the primitive roads. Undismayed, parents and children enjoyed card parties, dances, or movies at least twice a week, with Diablo residents often traveling to

Newhalem by train. Thomas Bucknell, a Skagit Project manager, remembered those trips to see Wednesday night movies. Seattle City Light parked small locomotives and boxcars near his house and, with Bucknell operating the engine, Diablo families piled into the boxcars. The trip was like a big party with families singing and drinking cocoa from thermos bottles on the way home.

Rifle clubs, Boy and Girl Scouts, and a "Mickey Mouse" club all thrived to keep the children busy. John and Dorothy Childs bought the first television set and invited local children to come and watch the one or two channels available. Supervisor Donald Hundahl fondly remembered eating popcorn and watching "The Cisco Kid."

Since 1972, sparked by the advent of more traffic through the community on the new North Cascades Highway, Skagit Project management has embarked on "Operation Cascade" to modernize and streamline operations, thus reducing staff by about thirty-five workers. They also removed about sixty outdated homes from Newhalem, most having been remodeled from the original World War I tent cabins. The newest addition to Newhalem was the completion of a handsome North Cascades Visitor Center a half mile south in 1993.

Diablo, at the head of Diablo Lake, was originally dubbed Hollywood because the keeper of the campsite was named Clara Bow. "Hollywood" later became the term for the portion of Diablo occupied by the executive echelon, and "Diablo" was used for the working families' section. Diablo as a camp served workers constructing Diablo Dam, beginning in 1925. The workers ate in a common cookhouse where, with little else to attract them to the remote location, City Light made sure the food was tasty and plentiful.

Most Ross Dam workers lived where Bradley's Resort was located until recently—a little beyond Diablo. Fishing was so good then that a man could catch gunnysacks full. A cougar hunter, Chuck Horn, living at Diablo hunted with a pack of hounds and brought in about fourteen kills one year.

The handful of residents of Diablo and Newhalem built a swimming pool with volunteer labor, demonstrating the unique community spirit that marked the place. The 150 or 200 residents find the wildlife entertaining, with bears showing up to enjoy downed apples and an occasional moose that sets up grazing rights on lawns and shrubbery.

In the spring Ed Scott hauled cattle to Diablo from his ranch at Marblemount, then herded them through the community and on up to Jack Mountain. The trail led across a suspension bridge near Ross Dam, always an exciting time for the herd and herders, some of whom were volunteers out for adventure. Adventure, indeed, for the trail was so treacherous that, if animals spooked, some were sure to fall to their deaths.

Bacon Creek Lodge. Before any residents lived along Bacon Creek, loggers came there to cut cedar shingle bolts (short lengths of cedar trees), living in a bolt camp seven miles up the creek. They dumped the bolts into the creek to drift down to mills on the Skagit downriver. Often local Indian men "herded" the bolts. Workers usually stayed in a camp, furnishing their own blankets but receiving board and shelter.

The once-popular Bacon Creek Lodge, five miles east of Marblemount near the junction of today's North Cascades Highway and Bacon Creek, was first the homestead of Francis M. Younkin in 1908. Younkin sold the homestead to Ed Horlick, who built cabins to serve fishermen and hunters. Horlick incurred significant debts and sold a half share to Joe Barta in the early 1920s to defray some of his costs. He later left the country, leaving Barta to take over ownership of the property in 1926. Barta expanded the original home, adding rooms and a big porch, carbide lights, and a pump for household water. The lodge, with four bedrooms upstairs and four housekeeping cabins—a bed and breakfast business—operated in summer only and was popular with fishermen. Barta's sons Franklin and Howard often guided fishermen to the best spots. Frank told the author that in the 1930s Bacon Creek enjoyed plentiful trout and large salmon runs. A neighbor, Native American Walter Sam, often speared huge salmon from the creek. The runs dwindled. "The fish just don't have the memory to go up there any more," Frank said. In a grass roots effort to save the trout, he and Concrete High School buddies hauled trout fingerlings to Jordan Lake, Lake Ann, and others in the 1930s. Seattle City Light's railroad ran by the resort across a long trestle and—when roads were clogged—sometimes was the only transportation. Locals gathered at the lodge for dances, and in 1934, the boys from the nearby Civilian Conservation Corps camp came to Mrs. Barta's small commissary to buy candy, tobacco, and so on.

In addition to Bacon Creek Lodge, which closed around 1936 to become merely the Barta family's home, a silica mine operated on a hillside about two miles upriver near Alma Creek. The North Cascades Highway bisects a second one about one and one-half miles east of Bacon Creek.

The infamous Bacon Creek Fire of 1926 started about one-half mile away from the Barta property. Nine-year-old Frank Barta was sent to alert Fire Guard Frank Oakes. The fire traveled easterly, jumped the Skagit

River, and ran unchecked all the way to Newhalem until rains extinguished it.

Marblemount is located at a strategic crossroads for North Cascades travel, near the junction of the Cascade and the Skagit Rivers. The town never grew much but has bumbled along in a relaxed fashion to remain a viable settlement today. Marblemount started a bit upstream from its present location on the claim of George Engles. (Engles was there earlier but did not file on his property until July 28, 1897.) Carl Buller came to the site in 1890 looking for a government claim. Engles advised him to file on a squatter's claim upriver, so Carl returned to get his mother and brother Richard from Sedro-Woolley. They arrived in Marblemount by river and trail. When they came to the site of Marblemount:

> a large pile of groceries were covered with a tarpaulin. A man with a pair of scales set up under a canvas fly was already doing a land office business in supplying the miners. About fifty feet down river a shake building with walls and a roof but no floor had a plank laid across two whisky barrels and was in operation as a saloon. My mother asked Frank Stewart, the store keeper, what was going on. He told her that someday this would be a large city. "What we need most now is a hotel," he said. Mother replied, "I am a hotel operator."
>
> —Richard Buller in the *Concrete Herald*, June 21, 1951

This sturdy, adventurous woman, Matilda Clark Buller, proceeded to build a home large enough to serve as a wayfarers' hotel, a busy place during the mining boom. (Buller was separated from her husband, a Civil War veteran with a drinking problem.) When miners Morgan Davis and Alec Adams excitedly called to show Buller marble samples, she declared the name of the town should be Marblemount. The marble was of poor quality, however, and was never developed.

Probably the *area's* first permanent settlers were Maggie and William Barratt, who homesteaded east of the river from Marblemount in 1886. They built a large home and barn, cleared the land, and were friendly with the local native people. Barratt built the first cattle ferry across the Skagit, as well as a small passenger ferry, and developed a profitable general farm. Maggie Barratt often acted as a midwife, delivering as many as sixty-five squalling babies during her career. The Barratt home consisted of twelve bedrooms, living room, dining room, kitchen, pantry, and an indoor bathroom where bath water was first heated on the big stove and then poured into a tub. The roomy home became a stopping place for teachers, fishermen, and a few tourists, including Mary Roberts Rinehart while she and her party awaited automobiles scheduled to pick them up.

The first building on Marblemount's current site was a wayside hotel, operated by Richard Green today as the Log House Inn. It was constructed around 1890 by Jack Durand and Henry Martin of the Colonial Mining Company (Colonial Creek), and was soon turned over to Frank and Mabel Pressentin (Martin's daughter). The property was registered to William Pressentin in the 1890s. "Ma" Wright operated it after the Pressentins moved on. She also had a dance hall near today's post office, but it burned down.

Sadie Cudworth opened a boarding house to serve miners and packers passing through, while her husband Hugh operated a saloon that subsequently burned down. Hugh Cudworth moved to Los Angeles to build stage sets for MGM Studios but Sadie continued to operate her business. Herman Rohde came in 1904 and, with Sadie as an investor, started a packing enterprise with the headquarters at Sadie's Place. Rohde packed with twenty-five to thirty head of stock, mainly into the Cascade Pass region. Locals remembered his comment that the only ones that made money were the ones that sold stock in the mines. Sadie's long-lasting business also served construction workers building the Skagit River bridge, U.S. government employees, and transients all the way into the 1970s. The indomitable Sadie died at age ninety in 1963. Her niece, Hazel Tracy, told the author she was renowned—among other things—for making lethal wine out of "anything," especially dandelions or apricots.

Paul Pressentin purchased the mercantile store of Charles Simpson in 1898, little more than a shack with crude shelves full of packaged groceries and salted meat. Indians transported the groceries by canoe from the railhead at Hamilton. Each canoe could carry one and a half tons of merchandise, for which the Marblemount store paid seven dollars a ton. The Pressentins sold staples such as flour, coffee, raisins, and beans almost as fast as they hit the shelves. It was not unusual for a prospector to buy 100 pounds of dried beans at five cents per pound. Coffee beans were twelve and a half cents a pound. In interviews with authors Maurice Helland (*Mount Vernon Herald*, September 1949) and Charlotte Widrig (*Seattle Times*, December 24, 1961) Pressentin said that by the turn of the century steamboats regularly came up the river to Marblemount and, as conditions permitted, to Goodell's Landing. Pressentin remembered Captain Thomas Brannin of the *Chehalis*, who had a terrible temper and was known to throw objects at his crew members if enraged. Brannin also imbibed freely of "rotgut" whiskey and would return downriver any time if the whiskey ran out.

Pressentin also witnessed a race between two of the Skagit steamboats, the *Josephine* and the *Lily*. Near Marblemount neither boat could proceed through a rapids, and the captain of the *Lily* stoked his boiler with slabs of bacon.

Black smoke came belching from her smokestack as she steamed upstream—and passed her rival with passengers cheering and shooting their revolvers. On another occasion the *Chehalis* ventured so far upstream that she couldn't turn around. The only alternative was to back down for several miles.

—Helland and Widrig interviews, material in *Skagit Memories*

Young Richard Buller opened the Buller Brothers Lumber Company about 1902, a substantial operation until it burned in the late 1940s. Buller rebuilt but operated on a smaller scale. During World War II the mill was declared a "Victory Mill" by the U.S. Government, its output largely allocated to the military effort—primarily lumber products for shipyards. Meanwhile, Rudy Clark (no relation to Matilda) came in 1903 from North Carolina to farm the property now known as Clark's Cabins, still in the family. At one time the Clark property ran from the mountains to the river. From about 1922–37, the Clarks operated the Glacier View Cheese Company, marketing large wheels of cheese.

On the Clark property a big old barn from days past was a popular dance hall for decades. According to Tootsie Clark, four truckloads of Civilian Conservation Corps boys would come to the dances in the 1930s. The highlight of these events was a midnight meal prized by the men: pork sandwiches, noodles, pickles, homemade cookies, and homemade ice cream in summer, or sometimes a big corn feed or oyster dinner. Popular bands included the "Three Blind Mice," three ladies from Concrete; and "Three Belles," an entire family. The Clarks provided bunks in the cloakroom, so tots could be put to bed while their parents danced. In the 1930s admission to the dance was fifty cents and the midnight dinner was another fifty cents.

The family lost part of its lands, including the dance hall and cheese factory, during the Great Depression, but moved their enterprises to the remaining property along the North Cascades Highway. They built another dance hall, enjoyed by valley residents until a 1970s snowstorm caused the building to collapse.

In the 1940s farmers and loggers built small cabins along the main street (now part of the North Cascades Highway) of Marblemount, haphazardly mixed with stores and small businesses. Some were the homes of mill workers at the Buller Brothers Lumber Company. Several buildings in use now were moved from their original locations in Marblemount—which tends to bewilder long-absent residents who return to visit their former home.

Rancher and Seattle City Light employee Ed Scott was the first president of the Marblemount Community Group that ramrodded the movement of the old railroad depot from Rockport to become St. Martin's Episcopal Church at Marblemount. Scott erected the cross, made of lumber from old-growth timber in the area.

Clarence Jones set up a shake mill in 1967 which was still struggling along in 1996, even with cedar becoming harder to obtain under current USFS forest regulations. In 1993, he also opened the Shake Mill Restaurant in a Quonset hut adjacent to his mill. Jones told the author that the shake mills between Marblemount and Mount Vernon once produced $30 million annually and since the work was labor-intensive, employed many valley residents. Other logging or shake firms no longer operating are Martin Brothers, C & A Logging, and Stafford Logging.

Across from Clark's along the North Cascades Highway the tiny Wildwood Chapel beckons the devout. The building was destroyed in 1975 by vandals at its Monroe location, but the Rudy Clark family bought, moved, and renovated it. Six thousand people signed the register in the chapel the first year it was open.

7. SEATTLE CITY LIGHT'S DAMS

Crucial to the building of the North Cascades Highway was Seattle City Light's development of electrical power dams in the upper Skagit valley, because the company needed a road to supply its dam sites. Coursing wild and free through the narrow gorge, the Skagit River provided a meager avenue into the gold country, yet frequently devastated the Skagit Valley by flooding. The settlement of Hamilton, in particular, was inundated again and again and the Skagit delta often became a vast lake.

Seattle City Light furnished a partial solution to flooding while following its own agenda—that of producing electrical power for the burgeoning city of Seattle. In 1905, long before the company filed for a permit on the Skagit, a power prospector, Charles Freeman of Anacortes, stopped at the Davis Inn on Cedar Bar to examine the family's crude generating plant. Impressed by the volume of water surging through the gorge where the Skagit River was compressed into a torrent only thirteen feet wide in places, Freeman sought investors to form the Skagit Power Company. Federal regulations required a firm to post a claim on a proposed site, then file an application for a permit describing the work contemplated. (If insufficient work was completed before the permit expired, others could and did file on the same property. Sometimes speculators filed on promising sites just to shut out potential competitors. For the Skagit River Gorge the result was a monumental snarl of superimposed claims which the county had to sort out, delaying any real progress.) The Skagit Power Company filed on Box Canyon, renaming it Diablo Canyon after its namesake in Arizona, and started work on a large dam under the direction of C. L. Milton, a Colorado civil engineer. To supply the site Freeman tried to improve the trail into the Gorge but was defeated by the sheer, treacherous terrain. After ceasing work on the Diablo site, Skagit Power filed other claims on sites from Newhalem to Ruby Creek, but sold them in 1912 to Puget Sound Traction, Power & Light Company, a subsidiary of a large Boston holding company, Stone & Webster.

A five-year battle ensued between Stone & Webster and Seattle City Light (under the leadership of James Delmadge Ross). City Light won the permit for Skagit development in late 1917. In January 1918, when the Seattle City Council announced its appropriation of $5 million to develop a power plant on the Skagit, the city's residents were horrified at the cost and the distance from Seattle. Furthermore, skeptics said, those leading the fight for a Skagit dam were the same people who built Seattle's leaky Cedar Falls Dam. Would the taxpayers' money dribble out through a new Skagit dam, as well?

City engineer Arthur Dimock established an outpost on Gorge Creek. He moved his construction equipment from road's end at Damnation Creek by scow one and one-half miles to Thornton Creek, then dragged it over a skid road to the campsite. The scow was unable to go upstream with the heavier loads, so the operator tied ropes to trees and winched himself up the river. Workers were housed temporarily in the abandoned buildings of the Skagit Queen Mining Company some distance up on Thunder Creek. Some lived in tents. In 1919, Seattle City Light bought the municipal holdings of Puget Sound Traction, Power & Light Company.

The search for a site continued. Consulting geologist Henry Landes warned that during the Ice Age a natural lake had existed at today's Ross Lake, and that large deposits of gravel probably had washed down the Gorge. Drilling confirmed the theory; the gravel was more than 100 feet thick! Drillers finally found solid bedrock for footings, and Ross went before the City Council to swear to the dam's usefulness, although it would cost $10 million dollars. The Council was convinced, appropriating $432,900 to build a wagon road from Rockport to the dam site, a small sawmill, and a temporary plant, all under the supervision of Carl F. Uhden. Elated Skagit Valley citizens viewed this decision as a major step toward a cross-mountain highway, but it was not to be. Uhden concluded that a railroad would be essential for hauling heavy equipment to the site, and a contract was given to Grant Smith Construction of Portland to build a line from Rockport to Diablo.

The Gorge Dam

A final permit was granted to Seattle City Light on May 27, 1920, to build a twenty-five-foot concrete dam at Gorge Creek with a reservoir, a two-mile intake tunnel, and a temporary crib dam on Newhalem Creek (to provide power for the site). The railroad reached Gorge Creek in the fall of 1921. To avoid dealing with the infamous, narrow Devil's Corner on the old prospector trail, the contractor built a bridge to the south side of the Skagit River; because the approach was crooked, the historic corner was re-dubbed the Devil's Elbow.

The railroad from Rockport operated with a World War I surplus gasoline motor car purchased from Fort Lewis. The twenty-five-passenger train became known as the "Toonerville Trolley." For freight the company used a gasoline-powered freight car, a three-truck rail flatcar, and a ten-ton flatcar trailer. In 1922 the railroad was modified between Newhalem and Gorge Creek to use electricity, furnished by three electric engines and a rotary unit at the Newhalem powerhouse. Weather vagaries were a problem, with floods washing out tracks or landslides covering them. In 1922 crews repairing damage in the Gorge found traces of gold in the rocks on the right-of-way and deserted their jobs to prospect.

The R. C. Storrie Company of San Francisco gained the contract to build the Gorge power tunnel and brought narrow-gauge rail equipment; to use the existing tracks, they added a third rail. Storrie's contract proved to be financially disastrous. The company installed big air compressors and eight-inch pipe at Newhalem to carry compressed air two miles to the jackhammers drilling at Gorge Creek, an expensive distance. Although Seattle City Light had first claim to the power output of the plant on Newhalem Creek, a clause in its contract with Storrie exacted a $500 penalty per day for delays in completion of the tunnel, not always Storrie's fault. When Storrie submitted a bill for $290,000 more than the original bid, it collected only $88,000.

Because the Gorge Dam was not finished for use by September 1923 (the original cost of $5 million escalating to $11 million), the citizens of Seattle grew restless. Newspapers attacked Seattle City Light for inefficiency and graft, and for building a railroad without permission. However, an investigating committee cleared all concerned of graft, blaming the overruns on the rising costs of labor and materials, bad weather, and so on.

Construction proceeded. In December 1923 the powerhouse was finished. Two generators were installed by Westinghouse of Pittsburgh, and delivery of two turbines was expected from S. Morgan Smith of New York. During 1922–23 workers strung 100 miles of transmission line across rugged country to Seattle and added direct telephone lines. When the initial switch was thrown on the two generators at the Gorge, every telephone in the USFS district rang, bringing all the rangers onto the lines. The problem was easily remedied; the USFS phones simply had a common ground with the generators.

On September 14, 1924, President Calvin Coolidge pressed a gold key at the White House to send a signal over the Postal Telegraph Cable Company's wires to the offices of Seattle City Light, and from there over the phone lines to the Skagit to start the turbines and generators humming. Formal operation of the plant began at 6:15 P.M. Pacific Standard Time, and Seattle received its first 5,000 kilowatts of power from the distant Skagit Project. These two generators supplied Seattle with more electricity during 1925 than had all other sources in 1924.

Another dam was needed to store some of the Skagit's water for release during low water periods. Seattle's power needs were rapidly approaching available capacity and Diablo plus Ruby (later called Ross) were part of the original planned project. In 1925 Seattle created a three-man power commission to supervise the pursuit of a three-dam plan —Diablo, Ross, and Gorge High. As soon as the Federal Power Commission license was obtained, James Ross negotiated an agreement with the Canadian government covering land north of the international border that would be flooded by Ross Lake. Seattle City Light purchased two additional 340-acre parcels in Canada to be held until needed.

Diablo Dam

Narrow Diablo Canyon near the Davis's old Cedar Bar roadhouse was a natural location for a dam—the site was only thirteen to nineteen feet wide at river level. With the added expertise of a private engineering firm, Constant Angle Arch Dam Company, the City of Seattle's engineering office designed Diablo, the largest constant arch dam in the world at the time—389 feet high, 147 feet thick at the base, and 1,180 feet long on the crest. When construction began on the dam and tunnel, Seattle City Light added an incline railway. For years thereafter the sturdy funicular railway towed incredible loads up 600 feet of track, a 68 percent grade, and a vertical lift of 313 feet. Material, inspectors, workmen, tourists—all went up the incline. A short stretch of track connected it to Diablo Lake. The railway is still operational today, used chiefly for tours.

The building of Diablo Dam went smoothly except for occasional high water problems. The builders let the river run free until it was absolutely necessary to complete the center of the dam, building instead from each side of the canyon.

Thunder Arm of Diablo Lake (Photo by JoAnn Roe).

Unfortunately, construction projects seldom are free of accidents, despite efforts to minimize danger. Scaffolding collapsed while concrete was being poured, burying three men. Following an old custom, work-ers buried a silver dollar in the dam for each man killed on the job.

Water backed up swiftly behind the dam—too swiftly, perhaps. In March 1932 heavy rains caused a flood along the entire Skagit River, putting the new dam to an early test. Seattle City Light posted

107

watchmen over its fledgling. Fifty-five miles downstream at the little hamlet of Lyman someone started a rumor that a crack had developed in Diablo and the dam might burst at any moment. Visualizing a wall of water rolling down the valley, the Lyman Fire Department blew its sirens and spread word of the emergency. Residents grabbed what they could and took to the hills; even a few downstream residents, most more skeptical of the rumor, departed for high ground. Meanwhile, towns closer to the dam—Concrete, Van Horn, Marblemount, Rockport—went about their daily tasks—the telephone lines were down in that area and no one had heard the doomsday rumors. Nothing happened, of course.

Looking across Diablo Lake to the northwest (Photo by JoAnn Roe).

James D. Ross
The dam was completed but, with the stock market crash of 1929, available money vanished. James D. Ross of Seattle City Light was caught with his Diablo turbines sitting in their crates at the dam site with no money for installation. He tried in vain to get federal funds from the Reconstruction Finance Company in 1932 and 1933. Four years after the stock market crash, the turbines and equipment still were not installed. Ross appealed to Guy C. Myers, Wall Street investment banker, and finally got the money he needed on May 1, 1934, through a sale of bonds. In November 1936, President Franklin D. Roosevelt pressed a key at his Hyde Park home to start the power flowing to Seattle.

It was clear that Ross's heart, as well as his head, was in the Skagit canyons. He persuaded the designers of Diablo to lower the main floor of the powerhouse so that visitors could see the big generators at work. An amateur naturalist, Ross imported exotic plants and flowers for Ladder Falls Garden (fragments still remain) behind the Gorge powerhouse at Newhalem. On the theory that plants eventually adapt to a new environment, he installed hot-water pipes to heat the soil for semi-tropical plants. He planted oranges and grapefruit and expected to develop a variety of pineapple that would thrive in the upper Skagit. Wherever he traveled, he picked up seeds or plants. From Lincoln's tomb he got several small oak trees, from Mount Vernon two trees he named George and Martha, and from Hyde Park two he called Franklin and Eleanor. Ross also installed a small zoo at Diablo, where residents and tourists were delighted by monkeys, tame deer, peacocks, cockatoos, swans, and an infamous butting goat. But one by one, the creatures vanished, victims of wild animals appreciative of gourmet specials in the wilderness.

Ross wound up in the limelight often—too often for some Seattle politicians. In 1930, a mayoral candidate, Frank Edwards, apparently flirted with the idea of getting the giant corporation of Stone & Webster to take over the dams as a private enterprise. After gaining office, Edwards summarily dismissed Ross on vague charges of extravagance, professional incompetence, and of building his own political empire. Ross did not deign to reply but went on vacation, out of reach of reporters. Led by attorney Marion A. Zionchek and supported by Hearst newspapers, a civic uproar ensued, largely in support of Ross. Mayor Edwards was recalled on July 13, 1931, after a vote of 125,000 to 15,000, and Ross was restored to the Skagit Project.

In 1935 President Roosevelt appointed Ross to the Securities and Exchange Commission. Stone & Webster officials were apprehensive that Ross would then make life difficult for private power, but Ross was

Seattle City Light's tourist train parked at Rockport waiting to take on passengers bound for Newhalem (Photo courtesy of Seattle City Light).

reported as saying that if private enterprise could provide electricity more cheaply than Seattle City Light, he would be plugging for them. City Light bought out Stone & Webster's Seattle distribution system in 1951.

A powerful yet humble political figure, Ross died in 1939, suddenly but peacefully, and is buried in a crypt at the foot of Ross Mountain at Newhalem. A Paul Bunyan of power, of great imagination and integrity, he had one foot in the North Cascades and the other in Seattle. He also had a flair for public relations, especially his initiation of the dramatic Skagit Tours, an excursion to the Skagit Project that became one of the Northwest's most popular outings.

Skagit Project Tours

Skagit Tours was conceived in 1928 to counteract the furor about the cost of the dams. When an influential group of women in the Women's City Club questioned the expense, Seattle City Light invited them to

see the workings. They were treated royally and were awed by the majestic mountain scenery, returning to Seattle to spread approving words
about the Skagit Project. Within a few months the company organized
scheduled tours with Ed Kemoe as the first tour guide. By 1932, the
tours operated briskly under the direction of Fran Scarvie, a handsome,
athletic man who continued to squire spectators until the cancellation
of the tours during World War II. Here's the way the average two-day
tour went:

Seattle City Light held three such tours weekly, each handling as
many as 600 people. Visitors drove or took a bus to Rockport to board
the bright yellow steam-powered "Toonerville Trolley." After a scenic
ride to Newhalem on roofed flatcars passengers disembarked about
4:15 P.M., were assigned space in tents or dormitories, and were served
a huge, family-style meal. After dinner, they viewed the powerhouse
by crossing a scary suspension bridge two feet wide above the Skagit
River, then returned to camp for movies and other entertainment. On
a typical evening the USFS ranger on duty lectured about the Gorge,
or perhaps Ross addressed the group. As darkness settled over the
canyon, visitors strolled through the dramatically lighted gardens next
to the powerhouse. From concealed speakers came strains of inspirational
music and out of trees came the recorded songs of birds. Few thought to
question why the birds sang at night. A changing pattern of colored lights
illuminated Ladder Creek Falls while the loudspeakers played such music
as "Ave Maria" or an organ solo. Filled with high romance, the tourists
went back to camp for a lively dance.

They were gently awakened the following morning with a special
hymn, "Singing to Welcome the Pilgrims of the Night," which started
softly and swelled ever louder through speakers in each dormitory and
tent. After a logger-sized breakfast, visitors boarded the trolley to Diablo.
Three hundred people at a time rode the incline railway to take a boat
trip on Diablo Lake. While the excursion boat nosed through the nar-
rowest part of Diablo Lake, music played from speakers concealed high
on canyon walls. By noon the group was back at Newhalem for lunch,
with background music featuring chimes. To the strains of "Aloha" passengers departed for Rockport on a wave of nostalgia and goodwill. It
was hard to find a single cynic. For about twelve years, from May to
September, thousands enjoyed these tours, paying a nominal fee
ranging from $1.50 in the beginning to $6 in 1941. After World War
II the tours were renewed, but scaled back to only one day. With an
adequate road to Thunder Arm, Seattle City Light removed the railroad
in the 1950s. In 1975, the tours were shortened to a few hours, starting
at Diablo, not Newhalem. Visitors provided their own transportation,

but the traditional large dinner was served in a dining room at Diablo. The tours still are operating.

Ross Dam

By the end of 1937, City Light's power systems were putting out 417,285,000 KWH annually, but this was still insufficient, so the city launched into building the Ruby (later renamed Ross) Dam, the third of the Skagit Project. Ross Dam was financed jointly by the City of Seattle and the U.S. government, because the dam provided flood control. The company's engineers designed it, modeled a bit after Hoover Dam. They used a private consultant, J. L. Savage of Denver, designer of the five largest concrete dams on earth plus at least sixty others. During the war years forty-three Italian prisoners of war labored with American workers on the dam. The project was divided into four phases: Phase One established a barrier 305 feet high, completed in 1940. Phases Two and Three raised the dam to 540 feet in 1949, backing up Ross Lake beyond the Canadian border. At this time, Seattle City Light took official possession of Ross Dam from the contractors.

In 1953, City Light paid the Canadian government $250,000 to flood 5,475 acres to elevation 1,600. Details of Phase Four—a possible raising of the dam—were to be negotiated later. For the time being, City Light agreed that the lake would extend only to elevation 1,600 and that the company would pay the Canadians $5,000 annually.

In January 1967 the parties signed a long-term agreement permitting City Light to raise Ross Lake to elevation 1,725 and flood about 5,710 acres of provincial land, for which the company agreed to pay British Columbia $34,556.21 annually for 99 years. In July 1967 Seattle City Light received the Federal Power Commission's approval to raise Ross Dam, but decided to wait until its economic feasibility was determined.

No action ensued on this matter until a meeting of the company and British Columbia provincial representatives in 1984, when the parties entered an agreement and treaty specifying that the dam would not be raised further. As part of this agreement the parties formed the Skagit Environmental Endowment Commission with four commissioners from Washington, four from British Columbia, and four alternates for each side. The Commission meets six times annually to consider applications for worthwhile environmental grants. About twenty proposals are received annually involving the upper Skagit basin. Grants have been approved for studies on rhododendron genetics, fishing, and recreation, as well as for educational projects for children and wilderness education. The commission will operate until 2066, supported by annual payments amounting to about $75,000–$100,000 each from both B.C. and Seattle City Light.

Before Ross Lake flooded the upper Skagit basin, timber had to be removed. Seattle agreed to pay the U.S. government $176,619 for the estimated 318 million board feet of timber. No homesteads existed along the river, although a few "hermits" lived in the mountains nearby (see Chapter 8). Access to the basin was virtually impossible. Seattle City Light advertised for bids, but no company responded, because logging equipment would have to be hoisted over the dams and cut timber taken out the same way—a terribly expensive, backbreaking endeavor. The timber lying immediately above the rising dam was sacrificed, an eerie conifer forest drowned and upright. Some years later, divers attempted to go down with air-powered chain saws to cut trees (which popped to the surface). The work was extremely dangerous and, after loss of life, the divers abandoned the idea.

The Decco-Walton company of Everett signed a contract in June 1945 to remove trees farther upstream at the lake's northern end. A low bid again reflected the difficulty of removing logs. The Everett firm subcontracted with a Canadian firm for removal of trees in Canada. The two companies had to build about forty miles of road between the upper end of Ross Lake and the Fraser River—a road capable of supporting huge Kenworth trucks with 16-foot-wide beds to handle 80-foot logs. At the Fraser River's edge an A-frame crane with an 85-foot boom lifted the logs and dropped them into the river, where they were boomed and transported by tug to mills—the Canadian portion to New Westminster, the American logs to Anacortes or Everett, a long distance away.

Two forty-foot steel tugs, the *Steelhead* and the *City of Seattle*, were hauled overland through Canada to the lake, as well as a 50-foot wooden-hulled tug (which sank in 1958). The *Steelhead* made a crashing debut. The truck hauling it hit soft ground and tilted, flipping the tug in a somersault to lie right side up but holed in the Skagit River. Crew foreman Jack Sherin hauled the boat to dry land with a tractor, welded a plate over the hole, and left it there like a beached whale until the lake would rise and refloat the tug. The rough logging road was also used to supply a clearing camp because, concurrent with the logging, Seattle City Light contracted with Morrison–McEachern–Decco to clear the land above Ross Dam of scrub, slash, and debris.

The clearing, salvage, and burning of the timber was a gargantuan task. Just one boom to contain logs extended 3,700 feet from the west bank to a gate 500 feet from the mouth of Lightning Creek. The gate allowed boats to go through the barrier to the border. Log booms reached 500 acres in size, and free logs clogged the waterway, a hazard to

Even as Ross Dam was rising, boats cleared away drowned logs and debris from the lake forming above (Photo courtesy of Seattle City Light).

company seaplanes used occasionally to transport key personnel or light supplies. To cut the partially submerged trees, a worker stood on a one-man float, nine feet wide on one end, seven feet wide on the other, and fourteen feet long. The nine-foot end was notched so the float could be closely lashed to a tree and permit sawing. Despite the obvious possibilities for accidents, none occurred.

The clearing camp was established on a huge complex equivalent to several square city blocks, consisting of many 90-by-300-foot log rafts bound together with cable. It included a floating dry dock, comfortable bunkhouse—seven single beds to a room—and an amazingly modern kitchen with such luxuries as an electric oven, dishwasher, and chrome coffee urns. All rafts were protected by canvas roofs. The floating camp was anchored at first just above Ross Dam, then towed upstream as cutting and burning was completed.

Weather was an enemy—not just the frequent strong winds, but also heavy winter snows that threatened to sink the rafts unless regularly shoveled off. Bears were pests. Whenever the rafts were unattended, they came aboard singly or in groups to break into the stores. The more accustomed to people they got, the bolder they became. When a bear sneaked up and grabbed a man's lunch one day, the worker quit. Cougars attached themselves to the camp, too, sitting like domestic kittens around the fringes of work sites, waiting for scraps of food. Even the mountain goats seemed to have their young near the camps—perhaps a primitive instinct that there was safety in numbers. The workmen occasionally spotted a moose or timber wolf.

Rules were fairly strict. The crews were fed well, but heavy drinking was banned, and late hours were frowned upon since workmen needed to be alert the next day. Three men were actually fired for playing cards all night.

A curious event took place on March 27, 1965, when the log raft started to sway and tilt so violently that men were forced to cling to supports. The lake broke out in two- to three-foot waves, although winds were light. At Ross Dam the dials on the powerhouse machinery went wild for a few moments. Jack Sherin radioed Newhalem to determine whether a big landslide had come down somewhere, but Newhalem personnel had felt nothing. The crew determined later that the time of the Ross Lake upheaval coincided with the devastating Anchorage earthquake.

Clearing continued as construction of the dam got underway. The site selected was ideal, with footings placed in a deep depression thought to be the bed of an ancient waterfall. To keep the river from inundating the site, workmen constructed a temporary diversion dam. After heavy rainstorms the barrier sometimes washed away. Engineers solved the problem by drilling holes in a series of rocks as large as two and a half cubic yards in diameter and stringing a cable through them like a necklace to hold the diversion dam in place.

Setting up the operations camp for Ross Dam was difficult, because little flat ground existed from the dam to Newhalem. Materials were

The face of Ross Dam during construction (Photo by Doug Albee).

stacked from Rockport to Ross. To handle materials on the job, an immense cableway was installed, operating over a 2,800-foot diameter and reaching almost every part of the dam. It was capable of handling up to eight cubic yard buckets of concrete, and other materials up to 28,000 pounds. Two other smaller cableways, a Ledgerwood and a "Joe Magee" were installed to reach the few places inaccessible to the large cableway.

Forms for the concrete were prepared at the little carpenter shop at the dam site. The face was cast in trapezoidal shapes to enable constructors to get a firm grip on the structure in the successive stages. The finished dam had a pleasant waffle-like appearance. The heavy masses of concrete required a long time to set because of high hydration temperatures (and if left uncorrected would crack), so every five feet in height the workers installed one-inch aluminum tubing to allow calcium chloride brine, chilled by fourteen huge refrigeration units, to be pumped through it for cooling.

W. B. Wolfendale was project engineer for Ross Dam. Herb Faulkner was the original on-site engineer, replaced after retirement by Charles Shevling. Because Seattle's wartime industry needed ever-increasing amounts of power, Phase Three immediately followed Phase Two. The onset of war gave the formerly tranquil settlements of the Skagit jitters, for it was perfectly logical that the Japanese might try to destroy the dams that powered Seattle's industry. Seattle City Light went to a complete blackout the night of the Pearl Harbor attack and operated the powerhouse by flashlight. A patrol was organized to make sure no lights showed anywhere after that on the dams or in the settlements or camps.

The overall safety record of the project was good, but Nature did her share to make trouble. For eighty days in 1943, the Skagit's waters were so high that they poured over Ross Dam—too much water for the diversion tunnels to handle. No work could be done. The river claimed a victim in 1945, when the Ferry Bar Bridge was being reworked. While a two-man crew was working at night to stack material, an overloaded, top-heavy crane toppled into the river, making a complete revolution and landing right side up thirty feet under water. As it fell, the crane ripped out the row of electric lights illuminating the bridge, leaving one crewman to crawl off the partly dismantled bridge on a narrow plank. He hiked to Diablo to summon help, but all that could be seen was the tip of the crane. The operator's remains never were found.

A small camp perched on ledges of rock blasted from the cliffs. A few houses were moved from the south to the north side of the river below the dam. Single men were housed two to a room in bunkhouses, the main bunkhouse being dubbed Dammit Hall, and a few small houses were provided for married workers. The front yard was the Skagit River. Wives usually worked in the commissary or kitchen. Each man worked twelve days and was off two—not enough time to get much farther than the Skagit Valley to let off steam.

Torrential rains in 1948 undermined the cliffs above the Ross Dam camp. As residents slept an avalanche roared down to wipe out four homes. Stanley Jones was listening to the ten o'clock news when he heard a strange rattling noise, looked outside, and saw a house going right on by. His wife had already retired to her bedroom at the rear of the house. Jones said later, "I yelled to her to get out. She went out the window with just her nightgown and overcoat on and was barefoot." She escaped not a moment too soon, for the same slide pushed the back wall of the house into the front. Nearby, Mr. and Mrs. J. E. Newcomb suddenly found themselves in motion, house and all sliding down the slope into the lake. A wall collapsed onto Mrs. Newcomb but her husband rescued her. Unfortunately Mr. Newcomb's father was sleeping and was crushed to death. The house

Ross Lake from the North Cascades Highway overlook (Photo by JoAnn Roe).

stopped 150 feet short of the lake. James A. Muir, captain of one of the tugboats, looked up from his bed with horror to find the door bulging inward. "I tried to hold it back but the slide shoved it in on my wife. The slide drove oil drums and a refrigerator on our back porch right through the wall. Then the house tipped over. I shoved my wife out the bathroom window and followed."

Not so lucky was the Charles Royce family. Royce said later, "I ran toward the bedroom where my wife was but I never got there. A stove just flew at me and everything went black." Jack Johnson was trapped for a long half-hour in his home. His wife was injured when the side of the building collapsed. Upstairs, the slide took off the roof but only gently tipped son Roger out of his attic bed. Coworkers, hastily pulling on clothing, probed the debris for survivors in total darkness, because the slide had disrupted the power lines.

The slide was a testimonial to the treacherous nature of the Skagit Gorge, where at least seven distinct avalanche zones between Newhalem and Diablo existed. Slides could dump 300 feet of snow, 80 to 90 feet deep, on the trail or road in seconds, or mud and rock in the rainy season. No wonder prospectors in decades past sometimes disappeared without trace.

One winter, investigating reports of a huge avalanche near Ferry Bar Bridge, City Light employee Thomas N. Bucknell (later Skagit Project manager) and a companion went to assess the damage. Bucknell braked swiftly in alarm when he heard a loud noise like thunder. He watched in astonishment as a man crawled off the bridge and up to Bucknell's car. When the man recovered enough to speak, he said that a concussion from a second avalanche had blown him out of his snowshoes and thrown him against the bridge railing. The blast almost blew him over the rail into the river, but he instinctively hooked his arm around the rail. Bucknell and his friend inspected the devastation. The air blast had sheared off trees sixteen inches in diameter as if they had been cut with an axe. Bits of cedar were driven into seasoned telephone poles as much as an inch deep. When the men walked toward the main slide, they crunched along on a carpet of fir greenery up to two feet thick, and the scent of evergreen oil burned their eyes and throats.

Ross Dam was formally accepted by Seattle City Light from the contractors on August 18, 1949, carrying a final price tag of about $28 million. The powerhouse was completed between 1951 and 1956, while the company proceeded in February 1955 with the last proposed power development project.

Gorge High Dam

Gorge High Dam was to replace the original Gorge diversion dam. The supervisor of the design office for this phase was C. R. Hoidal, C. W. Cutler was the project engineer from 1949–59, and Merritt, Chapman & Scott gained the contract for building the dam.

With all the experience gained from building the other two dams at the site, the work went forward without much incident. However, a brand new problem arose that was solved uniquely. The porous nature of the terrain at the site, which had bothered the engineers of the diversion dam, was solved by freezing the ground just upstream from the dam site. Workmen drilled a series of holes four feet apart across the river channel, 250 feet below the river level into bedrock, and into these holes installed three-foot pipes with one-and-one-half-inch pipes inside. The pipes were pumped full of brine, building up a solid wall of ice and gravel across the canyon to prevent seepage. Some of the holes were up to 200 feet deep and, for all we know, the ground may still be frozen there.

When the waters backed up from Gorge High Dam, the historic "Toonerville Trolley" was abandoned. Rails and ties were removed and the roadbed was inundated. As a substitute, the contractor built a narrow, one-way section of highway from Newhalem to Diablo. Years later during the completion of the North Cascades Highway, the State's construction crews widened the road, but had to leave the tunnels one-way because of the difficulty of widening them.

8. MOUNTAIN PEOPLE

The wilderness draws like a magnet a few hardy men and women who exult in a challenge, want to retreat from social contact, or prefer the frontier. The North Cascades were no exception and played host to a variety of such adventurers.

Early Pioneers

Henry Custer (Heinrich Koster) was one of the first. Employed as a surveyor by the U.S. Boundary Commission in the summer of 1859, he spent his free time exploring the extreme northerly wilderness west of the mountains, not under orders but just because he wanted to. He made three sweeping explorations around the Skagit River, and recorded his impressions in a forty-seven-page report to the Boundary Commission. His first trip took him from Chilliwack Lake, a mile north of the new international border, to the top of Copper Mountain, from which he could see Mount Baker and Mount Shuksan. He complained about the thickets and underbrush:

> You have to work with hand & foot, to break, or hold away the very elastic twigs of the bush [unidentified], which if not careful will give you such a lesson, you will not soon forget. Add to this a most disagreeable thorny plant with large leaves & red berries [devil's club].

On his second foray Custer retraced his trail to Copper Mountain, then explored eastward between Tapto Lakes and Whatcom Pass to the Skagit River. He was awed by Challenger Glacier in the Pickett Range: "Nothing ever seen before could compare. . . . All the glaciers . . . vanish before it into insignificance, in comparison with this closs [colossus] of glaciers."

His third and final trip before he moved on with the survey was by water. In a canoe paddled by Nooksack and Chilliwack Indians he came down the Skagit River past Big Beaver and Ruby Creeks, where he pulled ashore to avoid quickening rapids. He found a set of rapids so steep as to be almost a waterfall into the Skagit Gorge, and turned east briefly to explore Ruby Creek.

Custer's report vanished into the maw of government archives.

John McMillan came from Ontario, Canada, to prospect on the Skagit River in 1884, settling on Big Beaver Creek. With sparse findings of gold, McMillan started to pack supplies via the Dewdney Trail (Hope, B.C.) to the Ruby and Canyon Creek mines. He also trapped during the winter. He took a common law wife, a half-Indian, half-black woman named Gordon, but sent her home after a time in favor of formal marriage to a Seattle woman, Emma Love. Long after the gold rush, the U.S. Forest Service hired McMillan as a Forest Guard in the Skagit District. Some time later McMillan—whether still married or not is unknown—moved to Seattle but, when he became old and sick, he asked to return to his old cabin on Beaver Creek to die. His grave marker still remains.

Tommy Rowland, known as "a nice old Irishman," came to prospect on the upper Skagit in the 1880s. He built a cabin, barn, and root cellar at Roland Point across the river from Big Beaver. He became eccentric and told passersby that he was the Prophet Elisha reincarnated and that his cabin site was the "New Jerusalem." He told a fellow packer one time that he was commanded not to speak for three days and three nights. He claimed he saw gold at the bottom of deep pools on Ruby Creek and persuaded a diver named Benjamin to come with his diving equipment and explore the creek. Benjamin found only shiny rocks. Rowland eventually was committed to a mental hospital but escaped and returned to his homestead. Authorities discovered his whereabouts and brought him back to the hospital to receive proper care. The Rowland buildings were used by the USFS for a time as a guard station.

George Holmes settled in 1895 on Ruby Creek about a half mile west of its junction with Panther Creek and became a successful miner. He leased the old Discovery mine and reportedly took $7,000 in gold from it. One of only two black men known to be in the Ruby gold rush, Holmes was well-received by his fellow miners but was something of a loner. He died in 1925 in the Skagit Valley.

Glee Davis and his mother **Lucinda Davis** were true pioneer settlers along today's North Cascades Highway. With the help of her children, Glee, Frank, and daughter Idessa, Lucinda managed the Goodell
Landing store during the summers of 1893 and 1895. After a flood destroyed her homestead on the Cascade River in 1898, she and her family moved to Cedar Bar on the Skagit River near the mouth of Stetattle
Creek (a site now under the waters of Gorge Lake) to establish a farm
and roadhouse serving the prospectors swarming to the Ruby–Canyon–
Slate area. The original cabin was destroyed by fire in 1901, but the
family rebuilt a larger one and another still larger in 1907. Lucinda
charged transient miners forty cents a night for beds and twenty cents
per meal. A guest mentioned that the beds were very crude and that
many travelers were loath to stop there, but certainly there were few
choices in that remote canyon. In 1917, the Davises enlarged the roadhouse to eleven rooms. Frank and younger brother Glee gathered hay
in the Big Beaver Creek marshes and hauled it to Cedar Bar to sell to
the miners. They also managed to pan a bit of gold to augment the family income.

Having come from an educated family, about October each year
Lucinda and the children canoed down the Skagit River to Mount
Vernon for the school season. Lucinda supported the family by taking
in washing and working as a hotel housekeeper.

Meanwhile, the USFS took over jurisdiction of the lands in 1905.
The appeal of the Davis family for a patented homestead was granted
in 1917. Twelve years later Seattle City Light condemned the land for
the construction of Diablo Dam. Lucinda died the following year (1930),
after the family had moved to Sedro-Woolley.

Little is known about Frank's life thereafter, but Glee became a well-
known and respected packer for the USFS and mines until trucks took
over. He moved with his family to Sedro-Woolley to work as an elec-
trician until his retirement, and died February 18, 1982. During a
1975 interview he told the author of his troubles with the old Gorge
trail, especially Devil's Corner, where the first tunnel eastbound is
now located.

> I was packing in a Sibley stove [something like a modern freestanding
> fireplace], shaped like a funnel only about five feet wide at the base. . . .
> You could flatten one of those three or four times without hurting it. Well,
> I tied it onto a pack saddle and we got stuck under the low-hanging Devil's
> Corner . . . you know, where they had blasted through the rock. The horse
> started r'aring around and I grabbed her by the halter and held her with
> one hand so she wouldn't throw herself overboard, while I unpacked the
> stove with the other.

When asked if pack horses did fall off the trails, Davis said they did if they got excited and danced around too wildly. While he carried all sorts of odd things by pack horse, he refused a man who wanted him to pack a 20-foot length of rail to a mine. No one else would do it, either, and the mine owner had to cut the rail into 7-foot lengths for transport.

Seattle City Light constructed a replica of the Davis's old water wheel power system formerly located on Stetattle Creek and installed it at Diablo. The system would have barely operated electric lights for a cabin or an electric range.

Joe Morovits was described as the "Hermit of Mount Baker," living quietly on Rainbow Creek north of the Skagit River. He developed two or three placer mines about 1916, put in water power to run a small stamp mill and a small aerial tram to bring ore down to the mill, but realized little gold. He would stay in the mountains for months at a time, then go off to live in Seattle for awhile. One Concrete resident encountered Morovits in Seattle and said he was dressed in a fancy suit and broadcloth shirt, sporting a beaver hat and handlebar mustache. As he was a handome and powerfully built man, he cut quite a swath. While there is no proof, it is speculated that he spent his time in the city promoting investment in his mine. Oldtimers recall he was always talking about his "big deals." Years later during the renovation of a Seattle hotel, a trunk belonging to Morovits was found, containing his city clothes.

Quincy "Buckskin Joe" Eaton spent at least fourteen years on Bacon Creek. According to census records, he was listed as a resident in 1900. Born in New York and a former resident of Michigan, "Joe" claimed to be the brother of a United States Senator. The grizzled old man wore buckskin-fringed garments and a cartridge belt with a rusty revolver. He wouldn't allow men or animals around his remote cabin, seldom spoke, and lived on vegetables from his garden. The USFS closed their eyes to his presence on government land. He died in February 1914, as alone as he had lived. His body was discovered about two weeks later by a hiker who investigated when his dog howled mournfully outside Eaton's cabin door.

Frank Willis made history in the 1920s by driving a huge herd of horses (estimates vary from 30 to 100 head) over Cascade Pass to sell them on the west side. Unfortunately, ownership of some of the horses was questionable, and he wound up in jail. The actual feat was impressive, because just Willis, his son-in-law, and a third man drove the large herd over the long, largely unused trail in November. The men were caught in a snowstorm and early cold weather, and Willis endangered his own life when he gave his jacket to his freezing son-in-law.

Later Residents

Jack Kerouac was a late 1950s denizen of the upper Skagit River country, a popular author of books of the "beatnik" era and later of the "hippie" culture. Searching for meaning in his life, he obtained a job as a fire-watcher at a lookout tower on Desolation Peak for the summer of 1956. The USFS sent him to a fire fighting school for a week before he went to his station on Starvation Ridge. Although he and his friends often used drugs, there at Desolation he avoided the habit. In the primitive wooden lookout, he only had to watch for fires, cook on a woodstove, chop his firewood, and read. His only contact with the outside world was through the USFS radio. According to author Ann Charters in her biography *Kerouac*, he slept in a sleeping bag on a wooden bunk with a rope mattress. He baked muffins, played games, and wrote on his newest book idea. Charters wrote:

> Jack wrote at the desk facing away from looming Mount Hozomeen on his north, the dark, naked rock of Hozomeen coming to symbolize for him "the Void," with its clouds and thunderstorms, the two sharp peaks of Hozomeen looming in his window as he lay in bed, "the Northern Lights behind it reflecting all the ice of the North Pole from the other side of the world."

Kerouac's journal, "Desolation in Solitude," became the basis for his later book about the angels of Desolation who visited him on the mountain. He was quoted as saying that, when the fog ringed Starvation Ridge leaving Hozomeen protruding above it, the angels danced on the mountain. Loneliness began to set in; he had hoped from the solitude to come face to face with God but he only came face to face with himself, wrote Charters.

Kerouac himself wrote, "I want to come down RIGHT AWAY because the smell of onions on my hand as I bring blueberries to my lips on the mountainside suddenly reminds me of the smell of hamburgers and raw onions and coffee and dishwater in lunch carts of the World to which I want to return at once." After Kerouac left the mountains, he returned to Seattle and San Francisco. He was a controversial author and wrote more than twenty books particularly popular with counterculture followers.

Jack Wilson was an Early Winters packer, philosopher, and politician. He was involved in the building of parts of the Pacific Crest Trail and in touting the building of the North Cascades Highway. In his later years he was a large and vocal presence in the debates over whether to build a major ski area in the upper Methow Valley.

Jack came into the valley with his wife Elsie after working on Grand

Coulee Dam and loved what he saw, acquiring sixty-five acres of land along Early Winters Creek. The couple built seven cabins along the creek, acquired a pack string, and soon were hosting visitors from all walks of life. Wilson kept a pack string at Lost River during hunting season, so that hunter-clients could go that far by car and get into the wilderness without delay. Wilson told the author in 1975 that "there are more than 500 miles of good horse trails in the Pasayten country and surrounding mountains. One could go eight or nine years and never do the same trail twice."

Wilson was built like a lookout tower—tall, angular, sparse with a quizzical expression on his long face, his head topped by a Stetson. It was easy to believe one of his stories that his mule dropped into a mudhole so deep that it left him standing up. He loped, not walked, on those long legs, and his language in and out of the mountains could blister a pine tree. But he was a master guide, conscientious, kind, and eminently capable. He racked up as much as 2,000 trail miles in a year.

Among his clients were Governor Albert Rosellini, Judge Hugh Rosellini, banker Walt Straley, numberless professional and business people from Seattle, dozens of USFS visitors, politicians inspecting the proposed routes for the North Cascades Highway, and many others. He hosted and guided American Forestry Association trips and American Wilderness Society expeditions. With the latter were Mrs. Allen Dulles and Mrs. Marx of the Marx Toy Company. Wilson told of Mrs. Marx's wish to see a good lightning storm in the mountains. "She got her wish," he said, "at Three Fools Peak in the northern Pasayten at 8,300 feet."

Storms roll through the high country swiftly and with little warning. The party of twelve had left their horses to hike 500 feet higher up the peak. From there Wilson noticed a dark cloud ringing Jack Mountain and led the party back down. He maintained the best way to deal with lightning was to keep moving and spread out, not to stay near trees. One could do little else. The storm moved over the party like sudden nightfall. It was like being inside a king-size kitchen bowl, with lightning flickering all around the edges and deafening thunder. The storm moved on within ten minutes without injuring anyone, and Mrs. Marx could only say "WOW!"

Dealing with as many as fifty head of horses and mules, both for riders and supplies, was an art in itself. Wilson did not approve of picketing the animals because it caused too much intense grazing; instead, he hobbled green trail stock and belled "popular" mares, and the rest of the stock tended to stay with them. Only once or twice did he have trouble finding his animals in the mornings. They spread out to find the best grazing without undue impact on the verdant grasslands. During the tourist season he left his base camps stocked to avoid packing in items like cooking equipment. A typical camp for clients consisted of a fourteen-by-sixteen-foot tent for cooking, another for dining, and four or five smaller ones for sleeping, as well as a dozen or so two-man tents. Transient hikers or horseback riders were welcome to use the camps but were admonished to leave them as they found them.

His days were not without incident, mostly while packing in odd loads for construction purposes. Several of his colorful stories involved a big mule he called "Liberty Bell," for he named his mules after mountains. It managed to get between two trees with a load of lumber, got stuck, and panicked until the load was scattered. Another time a load of five propane bottles for a highway crew slipped under the mule's belly, and quite a rodeo ensued before the animal could be subdued. Wilson packed dynamite into the mountains for construction crews, loading the dynamite on one animal, the caps on another. He said dryly, "About the time you start getting careless with dynamite, you'd better sit down and take a good look at your hole card, because you're liable to get hurt." Unexpected snowstorms swept the high country, with parties awakening to a foot or so of the white

Pack animals submitted to strange and awkward loads.

stuff. Wilson said he had been snowed on every day in a year during his lifetime, including one trip with Tom Drumheller, a veteran sheepman, his family, and a Bellingham National Bank executive, when it snowed eighteen inches on August 1. The Granite Creek trail used by horsemen to cross the mountains, just as the North Cascades Highway today follows that same creek, was hazardous—full of mudholes and decaying puncheon that had been thrown into the holes.

Jack and Elsie Wilson loved the people who came to ride, and talked of how a group would be fast friends after spending a week in the saddle. Wilson told of a timid New Yorker, a loner who carried a microscope and gathered flowers and leaves to show Jack. Wilson said he had expected trouble, but had fun with this man. Another time a priest said Sunday mass beside a small lake, having brought the sacraments with him—what a beautiful place to have Sunday worship.

Wilson commented that in May each year wild sunflowers make the whole Methow Valley look "as if some painter went crazy with yellow paint," that lupine followed about three weeks later, and wild larkspur in the upper valley.

Wilson and his crews built and/or improved about fifty miles of the Cascade Crest Trail that later became a part of the Pacific Crest Trail. They packed and guided media groups such as Don McCune and a crew making a movie of the high country for the television program, "Exploration Northwest," and a *National Geographic Magazine* crew for an article about the creation of the North Cascades National Park. One of his memorable experiences was meeting Justice William O. Douglas prior to a guided wilderness trip for Douglas alone. Wilson remarked that Douglas looked him up and down with steely blue eyes and said, "I'll go with you into the mountains." He said he was convinced that, if Douglas had not liked what he saw, he would have gotten into his plane and left right then. Douglas was very knowledgeable about the flowers, birds, and animals of the North Cascades and a thoroughly agile horseman, despite having fractured twenty-seven ribs after a horse had rolled on him on a trail ride near Yakima.

Wilson had definite ideas about where a cross-mountain road would be practical. He was president of the North Cross-State Highway Association in 1960–61, and used his influence to take state highway personnel on trail trips to decide routing. He personally favored a road from Early Winters to Washington Pass up the east side of the canyon. He also was a vocal supporter of keeping the road open all winter if it were built.

Extensive avalanche studies were made by state-appointed experts, including E. R. LaChapelle. The worst slide hazards on the eastern slope were and continue to be at Washington Pass and Cutthroat Pass (where big cornices tend to form over the highway). Wilson urged highway officials to send someone to study avalanche control methods at Rogers Pass on the Trans-Canada Highway and in Italy or Switzerland. He stated that it would be less costly to continuously keep the North Cascades Highway open, blowing off the lighter powder snow accumulations with snowplows, than to force a way through hard accumulated snowdrifts in spring. He also urged the building of snowsheds along some of the avalanche areas, stating that if native shrubbery were allowed to accu-mulate on a packed dirt roof for the sheds, they would not become a visual wilderness intrusion.

After a lively and colorful life, Jack Wilson died in 1983, followed by his wife Elsie in 1990.

Doug Devin fell in love with the mountains of the upper Methow, endeavoring to hammer out a satisfactory zoning system to both develop and protect the ambience of the region. He operated the children's ski program at Crystal Mountain (out of Seattle) and was involved in other business enterprises. The Devin family were frequent guests at the Wilson Ranch. Hence, when Jack Wilson searched for ways to stay open in the winter, he queried Devin about the feasibility of clear-ing a beginner's ski hill behind his cabins. Devin thought the site was too limited but he and Wilson explored Sandy Butte one fall. The two men gathered information and formed the Methow Valley Winter Sports Council, membership largely consisting of Methow skiers, to look into the possibility of building a full-fledged ski area. The Council and Devin completed a feasibility study over a two-year period, publishing it in 1970. Bob Cram, the emcee of the popular KING-TV show "Ski Nanny," came to make a film of the exceptional skiing possible in the area. Wilson took him by snowcat to the top of a 200-acre cleared area on Sandy Butte. After skiing the butte, he was excited by the dry powder snow, the terrain, and the advantages of developing a destination ski area.

Wilson was as vocal in his support of the ski area as he was for the North Cascades Highway. In the 1960s the Forest Service and National Park Service made a complete study of all the possible ski sites in the North Cascades from Chelan to Canada, no matter how tentative. Out of fifteen such sites listed, Sandy Butte was named the one with the very best potential. Such publicity led to increasing enthusiasm by the Methow Valley Winter Sports Council, which assisted private owners in pooling enough land to make a ski development possible, an "Aspen or Vail" type of destination resort. However, Devin and the Council were concerned that the unzoned valley would be developed helter skelter and become an ugly strip development. They opened discussions with the county to create proper zoning to prevent this, while allowing an attractive resort development.

In the mid-1970s the valley received an influx of people fleeing the big city and seeking isolation and the country life. The newcomers came from Seattle, California, and several from Aspen itself, some retired, others living frugally. Many of these new arrivals equated skiing with affluence, while their thrust was back to nature. Most of the old valley residents sought new, well-paying jobs and regarded a ski development as an economic boon. The two lifestyles clashed, often in vigorous debate at hearings, and one of the most vociferous and colorful supporters of the ski hill was Jack Wilson—the man who had had the idea in the first place.

The opponents to the ski area formed an interest group called the Methow Valley Citizens Council, and obtained grants to finance strategies such as filing suits and appeals protesting the granting of USFS permits. While the proponents had interested developers from Aspen (a group known as Methow Recreation Inc.) in the Sandy Butte project, the delay in obtaining a USFS permit caused them to lose interest—especially after the British Columbia government wooed them to open a ski resort at Whistler-Blackcomb north of Vancouver.

Devin's efforts at obtaining sensible zoning and land use regulations were not in vain, however—they prevented strip development and took into consideration such matters as air and water quality for the valley and some protection for wildlife.

Enthusiasm for cross-country skiing increased. Sun Mountain Lodge created groomed trails, headquartered at first out of the Virginian Motel in Winthrop. Devin built the first cross-country trail at Mazama and talked Wilson into staying open in winter. The Mazama Inn and later The Ranch House opened to skiers. By the 1980s the Methow Valley's prodigious snowpack was becoming popular. Acting as a consultant, Devin assisted the R. D. Merrill Company, a Northwest logging and investment firm, in obtaining permits to establish Arrowleaf Resort on Jack Wilson's property. Merrill and others built the Freestone Inn and a pond, and improved Wilson's old cabins. Merrill presently awaits the outcome of appeals filed by the Methow Valley Citizens Council against the granting of permits for Arrowleaf's further development, which would eventually include condos and permanent homes.

Ed Kikendall and his brother **Chuck** were mountain men and Methow Valley pioneers. Kikendall's parents homesteaded near Winthrop in Wolf Creek Valley in 1910. Kikendall remembered Indians coming to dig rockroses and wild garlic in spring, later to dig camas bulbs, dry fish, and pick huckleberries in fall. After his father's death when Ed was eight years old, Ed ran a trapline as he walked between his home and school, catching coyotes, weasels, skunks, and rabbits.

When he was old enough, he sailed on tramp steamers around the Pacific and into the Arctic Ocean, worked on a whaling ship in the days of harpoons and cannons and at a whaling station as a meatcutter, and was employed by North Pacific Sea Products out of Seattle and at Akutan, an island in the Aleutians. Returning to the Methow, he and a partner trapped from 1920–26 in the Pasayten country, Canyon Creek, Rock Creek, and elsewhere for marten, fox, lynx, weasels, and other fur-bearing animals. They usually left in early winter riding ancient horses that they killed for bait once they arrived at their base camp on Skull Creek. They trapped until late February or as soon as animals' fur started to show black specks on the inside of the skins, indicating that the prime season was over.

Early one winter their main cabin burned, destroying all their packed-in food. The men managed to save their bedrolls and stayed in the mountains anyway, living off the game they shot. Big storms dumped as much as three feet of snow at one time, with snow turning to rain to form a hard crust on top. The condition caused slides that took everything off a mountain, including live timber. Temperatures on the eastern slopes usually would not exceed -10 or -20 degrees but around Hart's Pass could go to -60. Kikendall told the author about getting caught in a snowslide about 11:00 P.M. as he was returning to camp at Oregon Basin (over the mountain from Slate Creek): "The slide took off with me, and I slid with it. It stopped just over a ridge and threw me over the top. There was four or five feet of snow on top of me but it was loose so I could get out of it with my snowshoes intact."

Sometimes Kikendall would fell a tree or start a snowball to deliberately trigger a slide so he could safely cross a slope. On another occasion he was skiing down a ridge and got too far over on a cornice that started a slide. He had no choice but to try to ski down on top of the slide until he could get sufficient speed to move off of it. Kikendall shrugged off any exclamations about such feats with a disclaimer, "I've clumb trees with skis on."

It was no surprise that, when the Stonebreaker Brothers of Idaho looked for a dog team handler to supply the Azurite Mine, they chose Kikendall and his brother Chuck. The contract called for four trips a month toting eighty pounds minimum, with excess paid extra. If necessary, Ed declared he could carry that much on his back. On the first trip up the mountain with a dog team, the men were caught in a storm and holed up in a makeshift cave along a windfall with a tarp over the top. Some townspeople worried about their whereabouts, since they didn't arrive at Azurite, while others snorted that, "If a Kikendall is lost up there, it's too tough for me." Kikendall said later the only problem was that being holed up with dogs in that small space made the air "pretty thick." Kikendall's rescue of appendicitis victims one winter at the Azurite Mine was described in Chapter 4.

In summer the brothers joined fire fighting crews. Kikendall almost lost his life near the international border at Monument 83. Walking in to the fire on a rainy night, Ed caught his axe on a branch. It whirled around his waist to cut both arteries in his wrist. He and his companion, Earl Ervin, tried to stop the bleeding as they returned to camp. There they tried a mixture of charcoal, soot, and flour to stem the flood, but Ed passed out from loss of blood. Ervin hiked out to the first available telephone, where he summoned Dr. E. P. Murdock from Winthrop. The doctor rode toward the camp at a furious pace, riding a stallion and leading a mare, transferring from one to the other, but the pace was truly killing—the stallion dropped dead. The mare valiantly brought Murdock to camp in time to give Kikendall strychnine while he stemmed the bleeding and sewed him up.

When mining activity slowed, Ed Kikendall stayed in the mountains on trail building crews, a part of the crew that built the Pacific Crest Trail (working for both Jack Wilson and Hank Dammann). He, his wife Hazel, and their children operated a 160-acre general farm, as well, to which he later retired. Ed died in 1980, followed by his wife in 1996.

Claude Miller is perhaps the best-known packer of the Methow Valley today. He has worked in the mountains for fully twenty-seven years, longer if you count his working for his father, George Miller, and for Jack Wilson as a youngster. George was the regular packer for the Tungsten Mine on Miner's Ridge at Glacier Peak, bringing supplies up the Suiattle River or over the ridge from Chelan. In 1970, Jack Wilson sold his operation to young Claude Miller.

Miller told the author that the first year was tough, when callers expecting Jack Wilson would say "Claude who??" His investment in the sixty-five head of pack stock seemed precarious, but packing for fire fighters kept him solvent. The following year he began to acquire some dude business, and the rest fell into place. Miller operates much the same way as Wilson did, with a base camp of tents. He tends to favor the country around Spanish Camp and Sheep Mountain, and does one or two trips annually on the Pacific Crest Trail. Not active in politics like Wilson, Miller has attracted few celebrities but enjoys a solid business from the general public—businessmen, company CEOs, and foreigners (including parties from South Africa, England, and Belgium). The movie "City Slickers," where dudes signed on to herd cattle, has created a demand for that kind of experience. Miller has hosted at least two parties from Japan who wanted to "chase cows." One party helped a rancher move a herd through the town of Winthrop to high mountain pastures.

In 1973, Miller added a service to private camps. He and Dick Blue selected gentle horses and rented them to summer camps for Girl Scouts, Boy Scouts, Campfire Girls, Catholic Youth Groups, and others. In 1996, the team provided 200 animals to camps all over Washington. In fall they retrieve the horses, pasture them near Grand Coulee, then move the herd—occasionally across country in the old cowboy manner—to corrals on the Chewuch River at Eight Mile for the winter, joined by Miller's own pack string of sixty or seventy head. Miller uses mostly horses, only a few mules, and raises some of them. He prefers crossbred stock, often with one-fourth Percheron blood for good disposition, tough hide, and good feet. He maintains that some purebred horses have thin skin and hair, getting saddle sores easily, or poor feet.

Presently the size of parties is limited in the Pasayten, Lake Chelan, and Sawtooth Wilderness areas—twelve people and eighteen horses. Miller works from June 15 to November 1. He operates two or three parties at a time, so logistics are crucial.

Packers refer to accidents as "wrecks" and Miller remembers several. Near Buckskin Lake one mule in a pack string of eight panicked and fell over the edge of a steep bank, pulling three others with her. Miller still held the other four. He had to rescue one mule hanging by its halter from an outcropping, about to choke, and another sprawled face down and unable to get up. Neither the animals nor Miller were hurt but things were lively for a few minutes. His motto is that the unexpected happens any time, not necessarily the unusual.

Miller and a crew once were asked to round up some wild horses and corral them for the Forest Service. Miller observed that wild stock always runs uphill and stops on a high place, never the opposite, probably an instinct born of being able to see a predator from a vantage point. He added that they also prefer to graze the high ground.

Miller denies his importance as a packer, although he certainly is the largest operator at this time. He pointed to the real veterans about whom little is known today: Clyde Scott, Tom Graves, Hank Dammann, Roma Johnson, and Clint Hanks.

George Honey packed for the USFS, working from the Winthrop Ranger Station, and also acted as a smokejumper when needed. He supplied three- or four-man trail crews, as well as lookouts, with their axes, saws, shovels, tools, food, and supplies. The lookouts usually were local high school boys on summer jobs which netted them fifty to sixty dollars monthly plus board. Probably the oddest object Honey packed was a large engine, which he placed on a sturdy bay horse, then stopped every few hundred feet to let the animal rest. Occasionally Honey trained mules and horses for the Forest Service. Honey told the author that if he did not pack the loads to the satisfaction of the horse or mule, the animal would buck until he made it right, but that if all was correct, a horse or mule could pack a case of eggs on each side and not break one going over a rough trail.

Honey, who was ninety-one years old in 1996, remembered pack strings moving furtively through the Pasayten country during Prohibition days, when smugglers shipped whiskey across the border to a waiting truck by night. A legendary sheriff, "Pop" Hughes, relentlessly pursued the smugglers but could not keep up with the sheer numbers of offenders in the rough terrain.

Some early residents of the Cascades have left us little more than their names. **Pat Carr** was a squatter living in the 1930s near Billy Goat Mountain. The local ranger hired him occasionally so he could earn enough food money to survive. **Frank Arnold,** an Englishman, lived on the slopes of Glacier Peak, where he stayed on after the Tungsten Mine closed. He lived off the land and made a small salary as a caretaker of the mine property. He was found hanged, but whether by his own hand or another's was never determined. **Gilbert Landre** lived west of Cascade Pass in a cabin that marked the end of road improvements during the 1890s building era. Landre was a prospector and trapper. Glee Davis told the author that he would come back from prospecting and say cheerfully in a thick French accent, "I got pretty good indica*tion* but no min-er*al*." **Bernice Beebe Currier** and her father lived and trapped in the Granite and Ruby Creek drainages in winter. **Stan Oldow,** later of Sedro-Woolley, trapped for years and lived in isolation along Granite Creek.

9. Guardians
of the North Cascades

A special kind of North Cascadian wandered the forest after 1900: the forest guard or forest ranger hired by the U.S. Department of Agriculture Forest Service. Interest in forest preservation was sparked by Dr. Franklin B. Hough, a physician and historian. Concerned about lumbering practices in the eastern United States, he presented a paper entitled "On the Duty of Governments in the Preservation of Forests" to the annual meeting of the American Association for the Advancement of Science at Portland, Maine, in August 1873. Three years later Hough received $2,000 to make a study of forestry matters, coming up with a 650-page report that so impressed Congress that it authorized the printing of 25,000 copies for dissemination. Dr. Hough then was appointed as "forestry agent" under the Commissioner (later Secretary) of Agriculture but had little jurisdiction over forest in the public domain until 1881, when he was named chief of a new Division of Forestry. He was succeeded in 1883 by Nathaniel H. Egleston and Dr. Bernard E. Fernow.

A one-paragraph rider attached to the Timber-Culture Act of 1873, an act responding to land frauds, allowed President Benjamin Harrison to establish Forest Reserves from public domain lands almost twenty years later. This declaration has since been referred to as the Creative or Forest Reserve Act of March 3, 1891. Less than a month later on March 30, 1891, President Harrison established Yellowstone Park Timber Land Reserve and by 1892 he had created fifteen Forest Reserves containing over 13 million acres. His successor, President Grover Cleveland, added more reserves. In February 1897 those included the lands in the North Cascades Mountains presently classified as National Park Service, U.S. Forest Service, and Wilderness lands. The reservations were not without vigorous opposition by many Washingtonians who objected to regulation by governmental agencies perceived to be run by easterners ignorant of the state's resources. Representative of such sentiments was an editorial in the *Chelan Leader* newspaper of March 5, 1897:

> Never, since the days when William the Conqueror laid waste the whole of the land . . . has such robbery of public territory been perpetrated as that which . . . alienates nearly eight million acres of public domain from the people of the state of Washington.

Formation of the United States Forest Service

Nonetheless, forest management proceeded vigorously after the appointment of Gifford Pinchot on July 1, 1898, as Chief of the Division of Forestry—a man considered to be the father of the American conservation movement. Pinchot had studied forestry in Europe, because no formal forestry training courses existed in the United States. His division consisted of only sixty employees at the Department of Agriculture building in Washington, D.C., and Pinchot requested that his title be changed from "Chief" to "Forester," a title changed back to "Chief" in 1935. He was instrumental in having the Division of Forestry changed to Bureau of Forestry in 1901, when the administration of the forest reserves was split between the U.S. Department of Interior General Land Office and the U.S. Department of Interior Geological Survey. Management became unified under the Bureau of Forestry and with the concurrence of President Theodore Roosevelt, the U.S. Forest Service was formed July 1, 1905. Prior to this time forest rangers had often received their appointments by political means. That changed with the new USFS; Pinchot set out standards and civil service examinations for hiring rangers and guards. The examinations included practical knowledge of ranching and livestock, forest conditions, lumbering, surveying, mapping, cabin construction, horsemanship, computation of acreages, and navigation by compass. Some ranger examinations required an applicant to cook a camp meal, then eat it. Rangers were required to furnish their own equipment, horses, pack animals, and firearms. An early poster seeking applicants reads:

MEN WANTED!

> A Ranger must be able to take care of himself and his horses under very trying conditions, build trails and cabins; ride all day and all night; pack, shoot and fight fire without loosing [sic] his head. . . . All this requires a

very vigorous constitution. It means the hardest kind of physical work from beginning to end. It is not a job for those seeking health or light outdoor work. . . . Invalids Need Not Apply!

Among Gifford Pinchot's own guidelines stated during a lecture at the Yale School of Forestry were:

"It is more trouble to consult the public than to ignore them, but that is what you are hired for."

"Don't try any sly, or foxy politics. A forester is not a politician."

"Don't be afraid to give credit to someone else even when it belongs to you. . . . You may accomplish many things through others that you can't get done on your single initiative."

"Don't be a knocker. Use persuasion rather than force, when possible. Plenty of knockers to be had. Your job is to promote unity."

The First Rangers

Between 1905 and 1909, the USFS employed only a few forest guards to patrol the vast North Cascades, thousands of square miles described as

a labyrinth of high broken ridges, heavily glaciated peaks, and deep narrow valleys. Its mountains are among the most beautiful and imposing in America. It has scores of glaciers, fierce torrents and waterfalls, high meadows and virgin forests.

——Roderick Peattie, *The Cascades*, p. 79

In May, 1909, one of the first forest guards, C. C. McGuire, was given the princely sum of $300 to repair a sixteen-mile trail into Finney Creek from the Sauk River, which involved building a bridge across a canyon sixty feet wide. With any *remaining* funds he was to build other trails. Proudly wearing his badge and carrying a package of beans and bacon, marking tools, and a "how-to-do-it" book, McGuire set up camp in an abandoned homesteader's cabin. First he had to rid the place of mice. To make a frontier mousetrap he cut the top from a five-gallon oil can and strung a wire across the opening through a centered small tin can open at both ends. He tied two pieces of bacon on the small can, partially filled the larger can with water, leaned a flat stick from the floor to the top of the larger can, and awaited customers. Within minutes a mouse ran up the stick and, not being able to quite reach the bait, jumped onto the small can, which spilled it into the water to drown. Twice that night McGuire emptied the victims from the large can, about sixty mice each time. Nonetheless, more mice crawled in bed with him and others took residence in his boots. Eventually his trap rid the place of the varmints and McGuire could turn his attention to trail building.

Not only did the early forest guards or rangers live under miserable conditions, they performed nearly impossible tasks. McGuire found his cabin surrounded by seven-foot snowdrifts one time, as he returned from obtaining supplies.

A big part of the early ranger's job was watching for fires and checking land claims. Recreational activities were scarcely considered. Homesteaders' claims already filed at the time of the Forest Reserve Act were recognized, but a claim could be contested and often withdrawn due to lack of farming with "due diligence." Any citizen could prospect for minerals on public lands and file a claim with the county after showing he had put $100 worth of labor or materials into it. If he proved that minerals existed, the claimant could receive a patented claim. Later, such filings first were examined by a geologist who determined whether or not meaningful amounts of minerals really existed before a patent was granted. After a person had a patented claim, he could not be denied access to it, but the USFS had the right to dictate standards for access roads to minimize environmental damage. In later years, the government did not have to permit access by road, just access, and that might be only by air. The tangle of old and usually useless mineral claims is an ongoing problem.

The USFS also continued to battle political opposition in Washington state. In August 1910, Governor E. M. Hay, with the support of Governors Norris of Montana and Brady of Idaho, sternly rebuked conservation politicians at the National Conservation Congress in St. Paul, stating:

> I am as strong a conservationist as I can be. I am . . . convinced that the people of Washington are more competent to administer the reserve of Washington than any bureau in Washington D.C. . . . . I am for state conservation.

He continued his objections a month later at a conservation meeting at Spokane:

> Significantly, 95½ percent of Federal reserves are located in the Pacific Coast and Rocky Mountain States. The eastern States have had the use of their natural resources; they have dissipated them and now insist they have a right to participate in the resources of the western country. They maintain that the resources of the West should be conserved for all the people of the nation.

Nevertheless, the USFS and later the Park Service stoically maintained their mandate to conserve the nation's timber resources. Rangers not only watched the forests but also the grasslands. Before establishment of the Forest Reserve Act, neighboring ranchers routinely grazed their stock on government-owned land. Pending investigation of the effects on the lands, the Secretary of the Interior banned grazing on federal forest reserves in 1894. After on-site scrutiny by a committee led by Frederick V. Colville, it was decided that regulation to prevent overgrazing was the chief priority.

In the early 1900s about a dozen operators moved large flocks of sheep onto government lands under regulated leases. To protect eastern Washington wildlife from contracting diseases from the sheep, disinfecting stations were set up. USFS personnel built a dipping vat near Pateros by walling off a natural mudhole with gates at both ends and filling it with lime and sulphur sheep dip. A steam engine shot live steam into the water to warm it. As sheep came off the ferries, they were herded into the pool and forced to swim to the opposite end. Eighteen miles farther up the valley they were forced through a second vat of sheep dip before entering the high country.

Sheepherders and their dogs stayed for weeks in the verdant pastures of the Pasayten area (Photo courtesy of Okanogan National Forest Archives).

Working out of Pasayten Ranger Station in 1947, Stan Dick was a typical fire guard and monitor of sheep herds. His territory was vast—all the area around the East Fork of the Pasayten River and Hidden Lakes. He cut trails and kept track of the sheep drives; in fact, about the only people he saw all summer were the sheepherders. Paul Lauzier came in at Eight Mile and grazed down the East Fork of the Pasayten (the area was dubbed the "Eight Mile Driveway") and to the west. Tom Drumheller had three flocks that came up from Pateros to Gold Creek by truck, then grazed all the way into the Pasayten past Driveway Butte, the West Fork, and Robinson Creek. Charlie Treber ran sheep in Hart's Pass, Slate Creek, and beyond. Later Simon Martinez had sheep near Rainy Creek. Small operators were John Eder and Victor Lesamiz, who had Basque herders around Spanish Camp and Bunker Hill. A few cattlemen also held grazing leases on the eastern slopes of the North Cascades. Livestock operators claimed that sheep and cattle helped the forests by keeping down the brush, that the resultant forest was like a groomed parkland, but USFS personnel do not necessarily concur.

Mountain Lookouts

For the rangers deep in the mountains, communication in the early 1900s was painfully slow and erratic, but by 1925 a bush telephone system was established along most forest trails, ingenious and simple. It consisted of a single telephone line that ran freely through periodic insulators fastened to trees and was draped loosely through the trees—so loosely that, when a tree fell across the lines, the wire might not break. When a guard or ranger wanted to phone someone, he attached a small receiver/transmitter unit to the line, thrust a stiff wire into the earth to serve as ground, and rang the desired telephone number. The phones also provided a respite from loneliness for the lookouts and guards, who were allowed one hour each evening when everyone in the forest could get on the phone simultaneously to exchange ideas and just chat. Although there was a radio transmitter at Slate Peak, transmission was poor to certain areas because the transmissions depended on "line of sight." Even today this is a problem. Some older rangers nostalgically reflect that the crude old telephone system worked better than newer, sophisticated gear.

Until most were replaced in the 1980s by mechanical monitors, lookouts perched on their stools on key peaks. Fire guards camped out at Hidden Lake, Pasayten Airport, and Hart's Pass, a sort of forward battle zone from which they quickly extinguished fires and repaired telephone lines. Among the network of lookout or guard stations on the central to western slope of the North Cascades were those on Dock Butte six miles south of Mount Baker, Sulphur Point and Dillard Point near Baker

Lookout stations necessarily were on high ridges with expansive views. They are all but phased out today (Photo courtesy of Okanogan National Forest Archives).

Lake, Sauk Mountain above the Skagit River, and Lookout Mountain and Hidden Lake Peak toward Cascade Pass. On the eastern side of the Cascades, watching over the Lost River area was the lookout at Mount Setting Sun, plus Slate Peak at 7,440 feet elevation overlooking a broad area, North Twenty Mile Peak and Lookout Mountain monitoring the upper Methow Valley, North Twenty Mile, Goat Peak, and others farther north. The lookouts not only had to contend with loneliness and lightning but with fierce winds. Lookout Jake Peterson at Slate Peak sometimes descended from his tower to sleep on the ground, fearing the tower would blow over. Often during lightning storms St. Elmo's fire (a charge of electricity that appears as a round flash of light around people's heads, horses' manes, or wires) danced along the rails of the catwalks and down the support wires. The smell of ozone was heavy during storms, and a person's hair prickled in response. Small trees responded visibly to the concussion of thunder. Lightning was the chief culprit in setting fires.

In the early days the forest guard closest to a fire trudged in with shovel and axe, clearing firebreaks and extinguishing smoldering logs. Advance guards called smoke chasers were stationed here and there, ready to move as soon as they saw or smelled smoke (later reports came into base camp from small aircraft overflying the forest).

In the summer of 1910, C. C. McGuire, based at Diablo Lake, could see a fire only about three miles away across the river, but it took him an entire day to reach it, three days to put it out, and another day to return to base. For long stretches of the Skagit River there was no way across except by "go-devil," a cable strung across the river so a man could pull himself across in a cage. One of the largest westside fires was the Big Beaver Burn, an all-summer fire that consumed more than forty thousand acres near Ross Lake in 1926. Hubert Wilson, then a Forest Guard and later assistant supervisor of the Mount Baker National Forest, said the smoke hung over the area so thickly that the sun always looked blood-red. The fire burned unchecked until the fall rains.

Smokejumpers

Of course, no one person could dent the swiftly moving late summer conflagrations. Instead the fire guards often had to run for their lives. In the early 1930s the Russians had experimented with mass parachute jumping and David Godwin, chief of fire control in Washington, D.C., was intrigued by the possibilities of parachuting into fire areas. He had the Russian data translated, then persuaded the Eagle Parachute Company of Pennsylvania to furnish chutes and experienced jumpers to test the theory. The experiment was offered first to Region 1 in Missoula, Montana, but was declined. Region 6, with headquarters in Portland and covering the North Cascades, accepted the challenge. In September the team moved into an old warehouse at the Winthrop Ranger Station, and local smoke chaser Francis Lufkin was assigned as support man. The professional jumpers were to make sixty jumps into varying terrain to gain experience. Often they came to rest in trees. Lufkin's job was to rescue and return them to base.

After fifty-four jumps the parachute team concluded they had enough data and, on a cold and rainy day decided that Lufkin should make a jump. The professionals suited up Lufkin and gave him rudimentary instructions for landing at Intercity Airport. Lufkin was more nervous about his very first airplane ride than he was about jumping out of the plane. In a 1972 interview he said, "I just assumed I had to do it. They told me about pulling the ripcord after a count of three, to get my body in a good position, not to wait too long, and that's about it."

While the Stinson Gullwing climbed to 3,500 feet, Lufkin reflected on the early chutes with their long, hard, linen risers that slammed into a jumper's head and laid it open, broke noses, and cut eyelids. He vowed not to let this happen to him. The jump went smoothly and, after training, Lufkin became a member of the USFS's first crew in June 1940: two professionals, Chet Berry and Glen Smith, and two trainees, George Honey and Francis Lufkin. In 1941 headquarters (still there) were established at Intercity Airport near Twisp. Lufkin commented: "I used to walk for hours or days to get into a fire. In August 1941 it took less than 15 minutes in the airplane to get to this one, and we had it out before the trail crew reached us to take us out. A similar type of fire the prior year had expanded (by the time ground crews reached it) into a 100-acre fire that cost $44,000 in materials and man-hours to put out."

To facilitate small plane activities an all too short airport was established at Salmon Meadows in the Pasayten area. In 1945, Army paratroopers were dropped on the Bunker Hill fire from a C-47 but, when the job was over, the plane barely was able to take off from the short strip with the men aboard.

The smokejumpers had some humorous experiences, too. In one case, they jumped only to find the roaring fire was at a Girl Scout camp. Another time the smokejumpers, awaiting ground transportation on a moonless night, detected shiny "eyes" in their flashlight beams and promptly climbed trees to escape the bears. In the morning they found the "bears" were cattle with shiny tags in their ears.

After World War II the parachutes were more sophisticated and less likely to injure the jumpers, and experienced ex-paratroopers bolstered the smokejumper corps. More than five thousand fire fighters, jumpers and ground crews, battled a huge fire in 1970. So many aircraft were involved that temporary air traffic control towers were set up at Intercity and Omak Airports. During one day, twenty-three helicopters and twenty-four fixed-wing airplanes were in use. Eighteen aerial tankers dropped over a half million gallons of retardant. An F4H jet fighter bomber from California came to provide infrared imagery to fire fighting strategists. Fort Lewis, near Tacoma, Washington, sent 155 Army personnel and sixty-five vehicles to provide a field kitchen and other support.

Nearing the year 2000, fire fighters are aided by satellite imagery and other sophisticated technology, but men and women still have to extinguish the blaze. In fact, a new concept holds that some fires should burn themselves out naturally as a part of natural cycles of destruction and renewal.

Ranger Districts

The organization of the USFS went through several changes, but today the basic unit of the USDA Forest Service is the ranger district. Of the 594 ranger districts, 86 are in the Pacific Northwest Region which includes the North Cascades. Next come the National Forests and Forest Supervisors' Offices, 19 of them, including the Mount Baker–Snoqualmie office in Seattle and the Okanogan National Forest office in Okanogan. The Regional Office is the next unit, with the North Cascades area a part of Region 6 (Oregon, Washington, and Alaska) at Portland, Oregon. Over all is the Washington D.C. office.

In the beginning the USFS was almost all male and white, but in 1992, 39.7 percent of the employees were women and 15.3 percent were minority members. The first woman to work for the USFS in the North Cascades was Iva Gruenewald, hired as a clerk at the Okanogan National Forest in the early 1920s after working as a lookout for four summers. During World War II, 246 women were employed as lookouts in Region 6. In 1943 the Portland office reported that one ranger "has been able to employ a versatile young woman who can handle his string of pack mules, drive a fire truck, operate a fire pump, write shorthand and type his official letters." Women also worked as aircraft observers, part of the Aircraft Warning Service. Women were definitely not to fight fires but were hired to report them so that males could extinguish them. As indicated above, in the 1990s women constituted almost 40 percent of the USFS force, filling all types of jobs.

The Civilian Conservation Corps

The USFS received a different type of assistance in trail-building and maintenance during the Great Depression. Under President Franklin

D. Roosevelt the Civilian Conservation Corps (CCC) was founded on April 5, 1933, to take men off government relief rolls and bread lines by putting them to work in the forests of America. The majority of CCC camps housed 200 men, almost 70 percent of them from Washington state. Of the 73,339 CCC men, 3,830 were Native Americans.

The CCC program was not a "make work" effort by any means. The Corps planted over 100,000 acres with trees; improved 37,000 acres of standing trees; controlled tree pests on 1.2 million acres; constructed 396 lookout houses, 281 lookout towers, and 147 trail and fire equipment shelters; and strung over 58,000 miles of telephone lines. They also improved or built 85,000 miles of forest roads and 42,000 miles of foot trails. The CCC not only vastly contributed to the public's future enjoyment of the North Cascades Mountains, but also was a turning point for many young lives. A Vancouver newspaper declared that "this one movement has stood forth like a shining star."

A Corps enrollee had to be between ages 18 and 25 (later 17 to 28), unmarried, unemployed, and have dependents (parents or siblings). They signed up for six months with a possible extension for another six. Later men with no dependents were accepted. An enrollee received thirty dollars a month, clothing, bed, and board. He was required to send twenty-five dollars a month to his dependents, keeping the rest for purchases at the camp canteen. Leaders advanced with increases in pay to perhaps forty-five dollars a month. The men received training in a number of skills that were the beginning of lifelong careers. Illiteracy was attacked, and the literate could take advanced correspondence courses. Many CCC men were from big eastern cities and found the west to be everything they had read about—Indians, mountains, cougars, and bears. At one camp in the Methow Valley (Gold Creek) the men were regarded by locals as native sons after belonging to the Carlton baseball team.

Bob Crandall, a Washingtonian CCC, appreciated his good fortune in getting into the Corps. He told Allen G. Gibbs: "three square meals a day, bed sheets on the bed, all the clothes we could ever ask for, and they paid us. To a lot of people, that meant a great deal." Crandall added: "They [CCC] made people feel they were doing something of value and were wanted and useful. The CCC built up confidence in people, particularly in youngsters at a time when they needed that confidence." (Allen G. Gibbs, "Birth of the Civilian Conservation Corps," *Okanogan County Heritage*, Winter 1983–84).

A long-lasting legacy to the Okanogan forest area was the Salmon Meadows Lodge, originally conceived by Chelan National Forest supervisor P. T. Harris, as the center of a recreational complex that would include the lodge, golf course, new campground, a small lake, and a network of hiking and horse trails. Between 1933 and 1937, the "Cees" built the lodge and a warming cabin. A handsome log structure, the two-story building was sixty-two feet wide by thirty-two feet long. Newly trained and gifted "Cees" craftsmen hand-wrought the iron door hinges, curtain rods, and fireplace pot hangers. They also fashioned tables and chairs from trees. Lack of CCC manpower curtailed the completion of the complex but, in 1938, a group of Okanogan area residents formed the OKSKI Club, which cleared slopes for skiing and built a rope tow and a ski jump, Okanogan County's first ski facility. World War II terminated any such frivolity and postwar veterans wanted steeper slopes for skiing, turning to the present Loup Loup facility. The lodge was used variously until the late 1980s, when it was operated by Irv and Margaret Sasse as a lodge (sleeping bags on cots) in summer for backcountry visitors and in winter for cross-country skiers and snowmobilers. Sadly, it burned in 1994.

Present Day Management

The Okanogan National Forest became an entity in 1911, and was combined with Chelan National Forest in 1921, with headquarters at Okanogan. Since the area was so vast, the Winthrop ranger district was split and Pasayten ranger station at Early Winters was created in 1936 under Robert Metlin, head ranger, a big title for a one-man office. Metlin was ranger, timber manager, engineer, and fire guard, all rolled into one. Recreational involvement was minimal. Pasayten was restored to the Winthrop office in 1966.

The main ranger station of the western slope is and always was at Marblemount, although jurisdiction changed from the U.S. Forest Service to the National Park Service after the creation of the North Cascades National Park. The Mount Baker district is managed from USFS Sedro-Woolley. Several smaller guard stations were at Reflector Bar near Diablo (a central outpost), Rowland on Ross Lake, Granite near the junction of Granite and Ruby Creeks, Thunder Creek, and others. A station at Newhalem provided Park Service information and, in 1993, a new North Cascades Visitor Center building was constructed. In a 1996 interview Jim Harris, Skagit District Interpreter, told the author that only a small staff handled the work in 1958 when he was employed by the USFS part-time to fight fires. After he became a career employee, he often patrolled trails throughout the Slate–Ruby–Canyon mining area. During the 1960s young couples sometimes moved into old cabins and tried to live off the land. On one occasion Harris had to rescue a couple about to have a baby, when their old military jeep would not start in cold weather. In the fall of 1976, hunters brought in the body of a backcountry enthusiast, Mike New, found on Jack Mountain dead from a stroke. New had hiked and prospected for years and built a cabin in what was then wilderness, but when the highway was located it was on the surveyed route. The cabin was moved slightly and remained until New's death. As district interpreter, Jim Harris heads the Newhalem North Cascades Visitor Center today. Fascinated by the folk history, he has a store of local tales that he shares with the public through lectures both in the park and off-site.

Like Harris, Harold Bowers started fighting fires in 1958 for the USFS Pasayten station in charge of fire watch, recreation, and related activities. Only three permanent staff members handled the work—a timber man, a ranger, and Bowers. A few years later Bowers went to work on the Pacific Crest Trail, then a hodgepodge of unfinished tracks. The idea of a border-to-border high mountain trail began with Californian Clinton C. Clarke's article in *The Pacific Crest Trailway*. Since trail building fit into the CCC program, it was approved as a project and by

Backpacker along the Pacific Crest Trail between the North Cascades Highway and Stehekin (Photo by JoAnn Roe).

1937, 483 miles of the Cascade Crest Trail were complete (or at least passable). Bowers and his crew worked on incomplete portions, starting at the Canadian border, Milepost 78, and finished the northernmost portion to a point near Hart's Pass by 1966. By connecting several trail systems, the Pacific Crest Trail provided a continuous path for hikers and horseback riders by June 5, 1993.

The USFS was responsible for building the Pacific Crest Trail as far as Maple Pass, near Rainy Pass. Jurisdiction then passed to the Park Service, which changed the routing slightly so that the branch to Maple Pass became a dead end. Packer Jack Wilson, Frank Martin, Jim Abel, Jerry Sullivan, and others involved in maintenance of the Trail conceived the idea of a wheelchair trail to Lake Ann near Maple Pass, since the dead-end section was almost level. When they failed to get USFS funding, the forest crews, particularly the smokejumpers, decided to build it anyway, during times they were on standby for fires. Thus, physically challenged people today have their trail to Lake Ann, compliments of the crews.

The intent was to keep the Pacific Crest Trail at the highest reasonable altitude. This was a problem since parts of the North Cascades were only snow-free briefly each summer—especially at the head of Rock Creek. Also, since trails followed the contours of the land, up one drainage and down another, switchbacks were necessary but difficult to construct. They frustrated Bowers. "We tried to make them longer but some places there was only one way up and we had to go." Crews had to deal with bears getting into food and supplies or frightening horses. Inevitably, livestock accidents occurred. Bowers said one mule was hard to catch so he left its halter on. During the night the mule managed to catch its shoe in the halter while scratching itself, panicked, and rolled down a hill to its death. A similar incident almost caused the death of a saddle horse but the horse had sense enough to lie still until it was freed. Bowers also laughs ruefully about a mule that balked at crossing a small stream, lost its footing, and rolled over the bank. The mule was marooned until Bowers stamped out a set of switchbacks up the steep incline.

Another eastside USFS employee, Jerry Sullivan, had the responsibility of inspecting contractors' construction work on the Trail. He was often on horseback for fifteen rugged miles daily and one day rode forty-five miles. Sullivan was the rider who raced across the pioneer North Cascades Highway trail as a publicity stunt (see Chapter 5). He maintained that in earlier days the oldtimers consciously tried to ease the impact of horses on the environment by going directly across country to their destinations as much as feasible, instead of using established trails. He said there were few recreational riders in the Pasayten as

Along the Pacific Crest Trail near Azurite Pass (Photo by JoAnn Roe).

late as the 1970s, but in the 1990s perhaps 50–100 people per day use the trails, either on foot or on horseback.

The cross-mountain trails that led to the eventual building of the North Cascades Highway were challenging. Harold Chriswell, supervisor of the Mount Baker National Forest from 1957–71 (then headquartered in Bellingham), said the trail adjacent to Granite Creek was the worst. It went through a tunnel of dark, wet, overhanging trees for nineteen long miles. The trail often was covered by two or three inches of water and had terrible bogs; to combat them trail crews built puncheon sections—logs laid side by side. By the 1950s the logs were rotting and the trails poorly maintained for lack of funds. During an interview, Chriswell commented, "I remember horses getting into holes so deep they practically went out of sight. They would go threshing around and pieces of old puncheon four feet long would surface. Lots of horses broke legs." Dusty trails then and now were hosts for yellow jacket nests. Stirred up by the horses' hooves, indignant bees attacked anything warm-blooded, causing pandemonium.

Granite Creek adjacent to the North Cascades Highway (Photo by JoAnn Roe).

Bears and cougars were commonly seen but usually avoided riders. Grizzlies were a rarity, most of them killed during the fur-trading era. Riders of the Okanogan Forest side had plenty of grass for their horses but, on the west side, dense timber yielded little forage, and the USFS often had to haul hay to their horse facilities. The main herd of horses and mules was held near Ruby Creek and the Skagit River, an overgrown pasture barely visible today from the Ross Lake overlook on the North Cascades Highway. When Seattle City Light built Ross Dam, a clause in the Federal Power Commission permit required City Light to furnish ten tons of hay annually to the USFS, to compensate for flooding some of the grazing grounds, an odd provision lasting until 1957. The company amiably cooperated with the USFS, too, in transferring horses, hay, and supplies to points along Ross Lake by bringing them over the dam and onto boats.

As recreational use became greater, USFS personnel often had to search for lost hikers. Before registration of hikers going into the backcountry was required, people simply disappeared. In July 1951 rangers found a note tacked up on a tree in Cascade Pass: "Help. We are lost in a blizzard and out of food and only God can help us. The Perkinses. Dated March 1951." No one ever had reported any Perkinses missing and, despite a search of the area, no skeletons were found. The mystery remains.

Carelessness in the North Cascades breeds danger, indeed. Today wilderness rangers—always in touch with their offices by radio—patrol the backcountry to educate hikers and horsemen, check camping permits, keep the trails repaired if feasible with light tools, report fires, assist the injured or ill and call for help if needed—in other words, act as repair persons, monitors, and aides. For a time it was the policy to clear the mountains of debris such as mining machinery, and many old cabins were burned to keep squatters from setting up housekeeping. In the late 1990s, this policy changed so that more of man's history is maintained as a part of the total mountain saga.

Emphasis of the USFS has changed, too, with the thrust turning to forestry management and sustained growth and ever more stringent restrictions on timber cutting. Far greater importance has been given to ecosystems and environmental matters than was the practice in earlier years.

10. NORTH CASCADES NATURE

Known widely as the "American Alps," the North Cascades Mountains are an arbitrary designation of part of the lengthy Cascade Range that extends south to a point where the Sierra Nevada Range begins. The Cascades received their name from explorers Lewis and Clark when they wrote in their journals on October 25, 1805, about the cascades on the Columbia: "This Chanel is through a hard rough black rock, from 50 to 100 yards wide, swelling and boiling in a most tremendious maner." Most people think of the North Cascades as extending from the international border on the north to Snoqualmie Pass.

Within the North Cascades are wilderness areas, recreation areas, a national park, and vast forest lands—a governmentally managed complex mostly, dotted with islands of private lands, mining claims, and small settlements. The magnificent mountain country is anchored by Mount Baker, Mount Shuksan, Mount Challenger in the Pickett Range, and Glacier Peak, but a host of other snow-covered peaks thrust almost as high. Except for Alaska, Washington has the most glaciers of any other state. The heavy winter snowfalls also are responsible for avalanches that cause the closure of the North Cascades Highway from mid-fall to early spring. In 1989, a major summertime landslide roared down over the road in the Skagit Gorge east of the first tunnel, forcing highway crews to move the entire highway. Frustrated shopkeepers were prevented from enjoying the summer tourist rush for fully a month. The

Aerial view of the North Cascades Highway as it loops toward the Methow Valley from Washington Pass (Liberty Bell at extreme right) (Photo by JoAnn Roe).

slopes of Washington Pass (Liberty Bell Mountain) regularly spawn snow- or earthslides that must be cleared, as do the steep cliffs above the Granite Creek portion of the Highway.

In 1957 Cascade Pass was selected for an intensive study of glaciers because of its isolation. A U.S. Geological Survey crew directed by Mark F. Meier installed basic living quarters and scientific equipment near the South Cascade Glacier, about eight miles beyond road's end on the Stehekin side. The installation had to be able to withstand snow loads to twenty-five feet deep and winds to 150 miles per hour. The survey team measured total winter snow and water discharged into South

153

Cascade Lake from the glacier, and from the glacial lake into the Cascade River. The study showed that the lake had grown from two to fifty acres over a twenty-year period, and the glacier advanced about seventy feet annually. A preserved stump recovered from the ice was carbon-dated at 300 years old. Mining claims in Cascade Pass/Horseshoe Basin formerly owned by William R. Soren and Robert A. Rukke, originally staked in 1880, were under the Boston Glacier by 1960. Recently that glacier has been retreating again. In 1996, under Park Service geologist John Riedel, a small crew tracked the mass balance (the relationship between snow accumulation in winter vs. the summer melt) of four westside glaciers in order to predict water availability and other factors. The same group monitored the ecological health of streams and rivers in three of the park watersheds, beginning with Thunder Creek.

Flora

In the damp and precipitous country of the west slope thrives the mighty Douglas fir, North Pacific mountain hemlock, and silver fir. Prodigious stands of western red cedar prefer the lower elevations; some have been known to live as much as 600–800 years. White spruce grows at high elevations. Vine maple, a sprawling shrub, fills in the open spaces in the forest and creates a red-leaved fringe in fall. Within the western slope forests lies that disagreeable barrier to hikers and riders, devil's club, with its thorny stems under large, rather attractive leaves. Alder, mountain ash with its appealing clusters of red berries, Pacific dogwood, and other deciduous trees are found in the lower elevations.

On the more open and arid eastern slopes the sweet-smelling, red-barked ponderosa pine spreads rapidly, and more spindly lodgepole pine grows in virtual thickets. In the wetter canyons Douglas fir thrives on the east side, too; giants of this species can live more than 600 years but most average 200–300. At timberline are spreading whitebark pine and the exotic alpine larch, a beautiful belle that snobbishly lives above its conifer cousins, usually at more than 6,000–8,000 feet elevation. Light green in color, delicate in appearance, the larch is a deciduous tree and clothes itself in brilliant gold hues before shedding its needles in fall. Former USFS supervisor Harold Chriswell told the author the farthest west of the summit he had seen (from a helicopter) a stand of larch was on an inaccessible slope of the Pickett Range.

Ever-changing floral displays brighten the clearings and murky forest floor from thaw to snow. Even snow which lies in the shade sports an odd red algae that gives a blush to its surface. The dark forest quietly brings forth pungent skunk cabbage in early spring, followed by fragile columbine and pipsissewa with its delicate spike of pinkish blossoms,

Flowers abound in early summer along the highway at Washington Pass (Photo by JoAnn Roe).

Dutchman's breeches, ladies' slippers, and low-growing bitterroot (commonly called rockrose). The meadows of the west side change from glacier lilies, buttercups, and dandelions to white daisies, blue daisies, foxglove spikes in pinks or purples in cutover or open areas, showy lupine in blues and purple, wild stocks, and wild radish.

On the east side, buttercups appear first along with balsamroot (locals call them sunflowers), then blossoming shrubs like the service-berry and mock orange (waxen syringa), ocean spray, chokecherries, and wild spirea. Pink and white phlox, blue larkspur and penstemon, wild geraniums, and blue gentian clothe the sunny grasslands. In the damp canyons thrive glacier lily, white marsh marigold, monkey flower, gentian, and violets. In clearings fireweed runs rampant, and Indian paintbrush dazzles. By summertime tiger lilies mingle with the waving grass, as well as daisies of all hues, anemones, scarlet coral bells, blue-bells, and on dry slopes the graceful mariposa lily. By midsummer the high mountain meadows host heather, yarrow, oxeye daisy, and saxifrage, along with a wide array of berry bushes. On hot summer days wild straw-berries sweeten the air with their perfume. And, of course, fall spawns a display of yellow and red foliage.

Many North Cascades flowers have practical uses. The roots of false Solomon's seal, a sweet-smelling plant with tiny white starlike flowers, will seal a wound, and common yarrow also was used to heal wounds. Miner's lettuce with saucer-shaped greens and white flowers probably helped early prospectors to stave off scurvy. Another salad plant was spring beauty, a member of the purslane family. Perhaps the best wild green was dwarf waterleaf. Desert buckwheat leaves relieved headaches and stomachaches, while tea made from the flowers eased high blood pressure. When ground into flour, the fleshy tuberous root of desert parsley made a tasty Indian bread. The tiger lily bulb is edible when roasted, and wild onion was used just as we use onion today. The wide-spread Oregon grape, growing on both sides of the Cascades, has tart berries usable for jam.

Buttercups could be distilled into yellow dye. When crushed and mixed with water, snowbrush makes a soapy substance. The straight branches of ocean spray were used for arrows and spears. Native Ameri-cans wove the stems of Indian hemp, a member of the dogbane family, into fishing lines and rope. A milky substance exuded by the plant became a rubber substitute in World War II.

Not all flowers are beneficial to humans, however. Occasional stands of poison ivy are found on the east side. The harvesters of camas bulbs had to be careful not to pick the deadly death camas, its nectar poison-ous even to honeybees. A short, ground-hugging plant called steer's head, its leaves roughly the shape of a longhorned cow, also is poisonous, and animals became addicted to an alkaloid in locoweed that made them "loco." The beautiful larkspur is poisonous to grazing animals, and the common lupine can poison sheep.

The National Park Service maintains a greenhouse and small staff at the Marblemount station to experiment with plants for revegetation of old, worn campsites and trails—especially at higher altitudes, where plants generally do not regenerate quickly. To date sedge grass appears to be the most thrifty and resilient. Careful records are kept of the alti-tudes and locations from which seeds and cuttings are taken, to make possible reintroduction of vegetation into the same locale and to avoid introduction of exotic plants.

Fauna

In this beautiful and complex paradise roams an array of animals, some shy, others bold from the learned confidence that man will not or cannot harm them. In earlier years timber wolves were seen or heard frequently and a small population remains. Moose are increasing in numbers. One band often winters along Goat Creek. Backcountry adventurers occasionally have seen a wolverine, considered to be the most vicious predator of its size. Bobcats, coyotes, and black bear are common. Although not native to the area, elk are on the increase, and black tail and mule deer are plentiful on both sides of the range. Marmots pop up in Washington Pass to gaze in apparent astonishment at passersby. Smaller animals include muskrat, raccoon, beaver, mink, squirrels, pine martens, rabbits, and wood mice and pikas. Cougars, always present, have become numerous and bold in recent years. The handsome beasts were hunted unmercifully until mid-century by ranchers who frequently lost stock to them.

Only one known fatal encounter with a cougar has occurred in the North Cascades. Near the Columbia River in the Methow Valley, on a December evening, 1924, a 13-year-old boy walking through a canyon by night to a neighbor's home was attacked and partially eaten by an aging cougar. The animal was hunted down and killed. Grace Stafford, cook at a Skagit logging camp in the 1920s, told the author that a cougar once jumped onto the broad window ledge of her flimsy cabin, spitting and clawing. Perhaps it was toothless and hungry. Loggers chased it away. Man-cougar encounters have increased in the 1990s, probably due to decreasing habitat.

Such clashes led to the declaration of a governmental bounty on some species: twenty-five dollars for cougars, five dollars for bobcats, and one dollar for coyotes. When the killing stopped, the reduced ranks of predatory animals had lost the war and retreated to the wildest, most remote refuges in the mountains. Since such destruction ceased, these animals have increased in numbers.

While "wild" horses really is a misnomer, for they were not a different species, merely escaped domestic horses gone wild, large herds ran through the eastern slopes of the Cascades for a time. They competed for forage with cattle and sheep herds, so they were hunted down and sold as mounts or for dog food.

Black bear (in varying shades from black to light brown) is a common species in the North Cascades. With attention to proper garbage disposal, humans seldom have serious confrontations with bears. For several decades it was widely believed that grizzlies were not native to the North Cascades but, of course, that is false, for grizzly bears lived in

Black bears are frequently seen along North Cascades trails (Photo by Doug Albee).

forests all over the United States. Recent studies of Hudson's Bay Company records indicate that 3,788 grizzly pelts purchased came from the North Cascades from 1827–59, secured through the Company's forts from southern British Columbia to Fort Vancouver. Early explorer Henry Custer shot a bear near the forty-ninth parallel in 1859 and sent it to the Smithsonian Institute, where it was identified as a grizzly. By the time pioneers and gold prospectors came, the grizzlies were shy and elusive, their numbers so sharply reduced that few accounts of confrontations are recorded.

According to Park Service biologist Anne Braaten, by 1975 the grizzly bear population in Washington and contiguous states stood at only one percent of its estimated 1800s number. The grizzly was named that year as an endangered species. Among the habitat areas where grizzlies were known or suspected to exist was the North Cascades National Park and adjacent lands. Under the direction of the Interagency Grizzly Bear Commission, several governmental agencies, led by the Department of Fish and Wildlife, studied the area from 1986–91. In 1991 the North Cascades was designated as a recovery zone. The zone basically includes the North Cascades National Park, most of the Mount Baker–Snoqualmie Forest as far south as Interstate 90, the Okanogan and Wenatchee National Forests west of the Okanogan River, and some small state-owned acreages. Estimated grizzly population at present is still only ten to twenty bears, with just twenty-one sightings confirmed by biologists during the study, and about eighty-one more tentative. Since grizzly males roam over a large area, some sightings may be of the same bears.

Braaten told the author that a recovery zone consists of proper management of habitat, and that compatible human uses continue within the area (logging, mining, camping, and so on). She hopes that the population will at least stabilize and possibly grow slightly over a long period, since bears are slow reproducers. Females may bear litters only once each five years and more than half of them might not survive.

The program started with vocal opposition from many hikers, horse-back riders, and ranchers. The Mountaineers were split about evenly for and against the plan. Fueling the debate were rumors that the Commission had introduced additional grizzly bears to bolster the population, which Braaten declared had not been done—such a step first would be subject to substantial public process. By 1996, greater understanding of the program's aims had resulted in more positive feedback from the public. No adverse confrontation between bears and people has been reported and Braaten told the author that more people are killed by deer than by bears or other carnivores. However, one should not belittle the possibility of danger. Avoid contact, especially when cubs or freshly killed game are around. A population of ten to twenty bears scattered over thousands of square miles is not considered particularly hazardous, and the mandate of the Park Service, Forest Service, and other governmental agencies is to manage habitats that support animals native to a given district.

Flitting through the trees or pleasing visitors with song are numerous species of birds. On the west bald eagles soar, officially an endangered species, but becoming so numerous in Washington state that they might be taken off the list. Since the eagles wintering on the Skagit River constitute the largest group in the state, the Skagit Bald Eagle Natural Area was designated for a major stretch of the river above Concrete. At established campsites one is apt to share space with

Clark's nutcracker, gray jays, or "camp robbers," who hover around to snatch unattended sandwiches or fruit. Less frequently Steller's jays can be seen. Marsh hawks soar gracefully, watching for the plentiful mice below. The mountain thrush lives along mountain slopes, only retreating to the lowlands after snow falls to search for food. This handsome fellow is larger than a robin but is marked similarly, except for a white throat and black V-shaped bib; the female is plain. Robins, sparrows, swallows, starlings, blackbirds, and Bullock's orioles are among commonly seen birds. The great blue heron is a thrilling sight as it majestically flaps its wings over lakes, rivers, and marshes. The tap-tap-tap of the pileated woodpecker alerts the onlooker to its presence. Snow geese come in large numbers to winter in the lower reaches of the Skagit River. Small birds retreat to the lowlands in winter to hide among the evergreen shrubbery and search for food—towhees, juncos, and chickadees. Game birds such as pheasant and grouse are plentiful along the North Cascades Highway's grassy areas and north in the Pasayten, while many varieties of ducks and Canadian geese winter in Washington or live there year-round. Since the ocean is not far distant, larger lakes and the Skagit River host gulls.

More and more, visitors hunt birds and game with binoculars, not guns. In 1989, a volunteer from Winthrop's Shafer Museum, Dick Chavey, began to lead weekly walks to advertise the museum, stressing birdwatching and flower discoveries. At first only a half-dozen people showed up but eventually perhaps thirty appeared, did the walks, and had breakfast together. Today he does similar walks for Sun Mountain Lodge's visitors, a labor of love. Consulting with experts, Chavey has identified more than 250 species of birds, including rare sightings of white pelican, tundra swan, and black-necked stilt. He told author Jeanne Hardy (quoted in "The Birdman of Sun Mountain," *Okanogan*, November 1995) that his favorite was the common chickadee, because of its cheerful cry and its tameness. Chavey told me, "The trails at Sun Mountain are well adapted for almost any type of nature observation. The upper trails give a great panoramic view of the area, and a good place to visualize what it looked like 10,000 years ago when the last glacier receded and left behind the giant haystack rocks."

Fortunately for outdoors people, no poisonous snakes exist west of the summit of the Cascades, but in the Pasayten, Hart's Pass, and all along the eastern slope rattlesnakes abound. Few cases of snakebite are reported, however. Mosquitoes are pestiferous in early spring within the mountain areas, as are black flies in midsummer. Probably the most active insect annoying to man is the yellow jacket, very aggressive in late summer. It nests in the soft dirt on trails, rising up in wrath when horses or hikers disturb it. The yellow jacket is attracted to all types of food, especially strong-smelling items.

Nature Studies

Volunteers are an important part of backcountry studies. In the early 1970s a retired couple from Oak Harbor, Dorothy and Ralph Naas, collected about 3,500 plant specimens for identification by experts, recording the elevation and location of each. Another year Margaret and Joe Miller backpacked into the North Cascades as "Volunteers in the Park" to study plant and animal life in the Big Beaver Valley and adjacent lands devastated by the vast forest fires of 1970, and to assess which plants might be most useful for replanting. They made plots in the burn area, keeping records as to the thriftiness of the different kinds of vegetation. Such volunteers work without pay, only receiving some assistance for food and transportation into the areas. Colleges and universities such as Western Washington University, Bellingham, offer work-study programs for projects such as trail impact studies, and the 1984 agreement between the British Columbia provincial government and Seattle City Light (see Chapter 5) also sponsors studies. Recently spotted owl crews came from the Student Conservation Association in New Hampshire to count owls in the Park. They found few in the north, several in the south, and numerous barred owls that might be competing with the spotted owls for habitat. Association volunteers usually are college students from anywhere, who receive no salaries, just food, housing, a uniform, and transportation.

Park Service biologists began a study in 1971 of the lakes within the North Cascades National Park, 175 of them, including mere ponds. Carrying their camping equipment on their backs, Robert Wasem and Gordon Zillges inspected the waters, studying the chemical and physical characteristics of each. They collected insect and fish specimens for later laboratory study, and assessed the impact of humans on the bodies of water. Such studies enable the Park Service to decide how to manage these assets.

11. THE FUTURE
OF THE NORTH CASCADES
HIGHWAY CORRIDOR

Although businesses on both sides of the mountains would like to see the highway kept open all year, it is not likely to occur in the near future due to low traffic counts in late fall and early spring. Both the upper Skagit and Methow Valleys are lightly populated, and the highway professionals feel that the benefits do not warrant the costs. Furthermore, Ted Dempsey, Maintenance & Operations Superintendent of the Washington State Department of Transportation maintenance field office in Mount Vernon, balances each autumn the factors of potentially dangerous slides or avalanches versus keeping the highway open. He told the author, "I become concerned with the safety of travelers as the snow deepens in the mountains above. The avalanches that are most dangerous you can't see from the highway; they are far up above and come without warning, and there are lots of those potential avalanche areas." His jurisdiction only goes as far as the Granite Creek bridge. For the west side the Skagit Gorge always has potential for rockslides or avalanches, and another bad point is around Ruby Mountain, a short distance east of the Ross Lake overlook. Toward highway closure time the Department of Transportation removes the guard rails in probable avalanche paths so the slides can continue right on into the opposite canyon. Otherwise a slide would pile up against the rail

The North Cascades Highway near Washington Pass is often choked by early winter snows (Photo by JoAnn Roe).

or sweep rails away into the canyons, creating unsightly debris that would be difficult to remove.

The most recent spectacular rockslide came down on August 15, 1989, opposite Gorge Lake in the Skagit Gorge, carrying boulders the size of a house. The volume of the slide was considerable. It overwhelmed the road and closed the North Cascades Highway until mid-September, to the distress of merchants and travelers. The slide left a ledge of unstable rock hanging above, inhibiting immediate repair work on the road. First crawler-type machines had to go in above the ledge, drill holes in it, and place explosives to bring down the dangerous overhang. After the work site was stabilized, crews opened the road in about two weeks.

The worst hazard on the east side is always at Washington Pass below Liberty Bell Mountain, where snowbanks linger long after the rest of the road is open. Furthermore, a slide here is especially dangerous to passing vehicles because of the almost vertical drop on the "down" side of

The precipitous slope of Liberty Bell Mountain encourages frequent snow slides. Highway crews keep the road cleared as late as reasonably possible (Photo by JoAnn Roe).

the highway opposite Liberty Bell. Near Cutthroat Pass is another major avalanche area.

Snowslides or avalanches are caused by (1) loose snow that piles up and starts to move, (2) cohesive snow which fractures catastrophically to become a "slab avalanche," and (3) wind, often called the architect of avalanches, since strong winds transport snow from the windward to leeward slopes quickly to become overloaded. The Department of Transportation is concerned enough about avalanche hazards that most employees are required to take an Avalanche Awareness Course conducted by the Department's Avalanche Control Division. Avalanches typically take place on the colder eastern slopes, with rockslides more prevalent on the west. During the winter of 1971–72 experts recorded 102 avalanches between Early Winters and Washington Pass that went as far as or over the Highway. The study group prepared avalanche atlases and diagrams for the entire mountainous portion of the road, numbering and depicting on a chart each potential slide area. Such studies may be reviewed at the Department of Transportation office in Mount Vernon.

Floods have taken a few bites out of the North Cascades Highway, too, especially in 1995, when the Skagit River inundated the entire road for about four hundred feet at Sutter Park east of Rockport.

Other than routine maintenance, no major revisions of the Highway from Marblemount to Winthrop are contemplated in the near future, except for replacement of the bridge across Damnation Creek between Marblemount and Newhalem.

Although portions have been updated, in 1988 the Park Service published a General Management Plan for the North Cascades National Park. The main points of the plan are:

The Park Service will preserve the wild character of the national park and recreation areas and help visitors gain inspiration, knowledge, and recreation from their visits in the mountains.

No extensive facilities are needed or even desirable to help visitors take advantage of the abundant recreational opportunities. However, Park Service staff will strive to assist people in becoming more aware of their surroundings by various educational means. The only major change scheduled in the plan was the construction of a new visitor center at Newhalem, completed in 1993.

Resource management will include protection of ecological processes (such as natural fire, native insect infestations, and stream meanderings) to maintain the greatest natural diversity in habitat. The Park Service will protect lands and waters in certain zones and will attempt to revegetate overused areas. It will consider issues of rare, threatened, endangered, and sensitive bird and mammal populations. Of particular concern is the grizzly bear.

An extensive visitor interpretation program will be (and is being) pursued, including wilderness as an asset, the natural forces shaping the mountains, environmental matters, history of the area—miners, trappers, homesteaders—and critical relationships between people and their environment, including those outside the park. Ninety percent of the visitors stay within the North Cascades Highway corridor (plus Mount Baker and other highways), and most of the visitor programs occur along these avenues.

Cooperation among the Park Service, Forest Service, Seattle City Light, and highway personnel is crucial to the health of the North Cascades.

Major changes in forest management have taken place since the 1990 Forest Service plan, which called for a mixture of timber harvest, preservation, and conservation, with restraints including the wilderness areas managed. Revised in 1994, the plan considers seriously the factors of the northern spotted owls and murrelets as endangered species, plus the need to consider the health of streams for fish habitat. The owl is the instigator of stricter regulations, considered the indicator of multiple old-growth dependency species. Large areas called Late Successional Reserves were withdrawn from timber harvest, constituting 49 percent of the Mount Baker Ranger District within which the North Cascades Highway corridor is located (plus other areas farther south not covered in this book). The spotted owl studies were led by Jack Ward Thomas (now retired), Chief of the USFS, Washington, D.C. The study group came up with a set of recommendations that became the environmental impact statement for the forest. The study was conducted in conjunction with the Bureau of Land Management and became known as the Northwest Forest Plan.

Jon Vanderheyden, Head Ranger of the Mount Baker Ranger District, said that before the 1994 Late Successional Reserves, 37 percent of the land was congressionally withdrawn for wilderness area. That has not changed. Another 7 percent is administratively withdrawn, leaving 7 percent (37,406 acres) of the Mount Baker Ranger District available for other purposes, including timber harvest—although smaller portions such as 4,000 acres for the Mount Baker Recreation Area are located in that 7 percent remainder. This management direction is for an indefinite period, unless the theory of management is adjusted by Congress. However, the Forest Service automatically has a ten-year review of its policies, so the matter might be taken up in either 2000 or 2004 (the original 10-year review took place in 1990).

Vanderheyden said that fire is still a predominant method of changing the forest. Different parts are more prone to fire than others, among them the south-facing slopes along the highway corridor. Hurricanes such as those of 1962 and 1990 create widespread blowdowns, and if more than ten acres are downed in one place, salvage might be considered in withdrawn areas.

The USFS also monitors the portions of the Skagit River and tributaries Sauk, Suiattle, and Cascade designated as a Wild and Scenic River in 1978. The Skagit was the only river so designated in Washington state until the late 1990s, when two small tributaries of the Columbia River—the Klickitat and White Salmon—were added. As part of the plan, government funds plus grants from Seattle City Light will result in the early development of boat launching facilities near the junction of the Cascade Pass Road and the North Cascades Highway.

Bibliography

Alt, David D. and Donald W. Hyndman. *Roadside Geology of Washington*. Missoula: Mountain Press Publishing Company, 1984.

Barron, Mark. Private history of the Sunny M Ranch.

Blonk, Hu. "You Ought to Write Her Up, Say Friends of Dorothea Albin." *Wenatchee World*, October 1, 1959.

Brockman, C. Frank. "A Park for the North Cascades." *American Forests*, September 1966.

Buller, Richard. *Concrete Herald*, June 21, 1951.

Chalcraft, E. P. *Seattle Post-Intelligencer*, September, 1957.

Charters, Ann. *Kerouac*. San Francisco: Straight Arrow Books, 1973.

Clark, Ella E. *Indian Legends of the Pacific Northwest*. Berkeley: University of California Press, 1953.

Collins, June McCormick. *Valley of the Spirits*. Seattle: University of Washington Press, 1980.

Custer, Henry. Report to the Boundary Commission. 1859. Quoted by John C. Miles, *Koma Kulshan* (Seattle: The Mountaineers, 1984), p. 230, n.1.

Daily Alta of California (San Francisco), 1858

Duffy, Barbara, and Marjory White. "Winthrop History." Typescript, January 1990.

Dwelley, Charles, ed. *Skagit Memories*. Mount Vernon, Wash.: Skagit County Historical Society, 1979.

Easterbrook, Don J. and David A. Rahm. *Landforms of Washington*. Bellingham: Western Washington State College, 1970.

Editorial. *Chelan Leader*, March 5, 1897.

Field, Newton, comp. *The Mt. Baker Almanac, Mt. Baker National Forest*. Department of the Interior, U.S. Forest Service, 1950.

Frisbee, Walter. Letter to Guy Waring. August 7, 1893.

Gibbs, Allen G. "Birth of the Civilian Conservation Corps." *Okanogan County Heritage*, Winter 1983–84.

———. "Salmon Meadows Lodge: A legacy in the forest." *Okanogan County Heritage*, Winter 1987–88.

Goudie, Andrew. *Environmental Change*. Oxford: Clarendon Press, 1983.

Hardy, Jeanne. "The Birdman of Sun Mountain." *Okanogan*, November 1995, p. 5.

History Line. Newsletter of the Forest Service History Program, various.

Hitchman, Robert. *Place Names of Washington*. Tacoma: Washington State Historical Society, 1985.

Horn, Mrs. Richard. "Azurite Bride's Diary." *Okanogan County Heritage*, Winter 1974–75.

Hough, Dr. Franklin B. "On the Duty of Governments in the Preservation of Forests." Paper presented at annual meeting of the American Association for the Advancement of Science at Portland, Maine, August 1873.

House of Representatives (U.S.). "Report of the Secretary of War communicating the Several Pacific Railroad Explorations," 33rd Cong., 1st sess.,1855. House Doc. 129, Serial 736, pp. 147 ff.

Jordan, Ray. *Yarns of the Skagit Country*. Sedro-Woolley, Wash., 1974.

Kerouac, Jack. "Desolation in Solitude." Private journal.

LaChapelle, E. R., C. B. Brown, and R. J. Evans, Department of Field Engineering, University of Washington. Paper prepared for Washington State Highway Commission, September 1972.

Methow Valley Journal. Shafer Museum and Winthrop Public Library, Winthrop, Wash., selected editions 1912–42.

Methow Valley News, April 1904 and October 1905.

Mierendorf, Robert R. "Chert Procurement in the Upper Skagit River, etc." U.S. Department of the Interior, North Cascades National Park Service Complex, 1993.

Miles, John C. *Koma Kulshan*. Seattle: The Mountaineers, 1984.

Murray, Keith A. "Building a Wagon Road Through the Northern Cascade Mountains." *Pacific Northwest Quarterly*, April 1965, p. 49.

National Park Service. General Management Plan for the North Cascades National Park, 1988.

Northwest Discovery, Vol. 3, No. 1, March 1982. "An Army Expedition Across the North Cascades in August 1882."

Northwest Discovery, Vol.3, No. 2, Sept. 1982. "The Pierce Expedition of 1882."

Northwest Discovery. Vol. 1, No. 3, August 1980. "The First Crossing of the North Cascades."

Okanogan County Heritage. Okanogan, Wash.: Okanogan County Historical Society, selected editions.

"Old Flint" [pseud.]. "Across the Cascades on Horseback." *The Sunday American-Reveille* (Bellingham, Wash.), September 1, 1907.

Park, Edwards. "Washington Wilderness, the North Cascades." *National Geographic Magazine*, March 1961.

Peattie, Roderick, ed. *The Cascades*. New York: Vanguard Press, 1949.

Pierce, Lt. Henry M. *Report of an Expedition from Fort Colville to Puget Sound, Washington Territory, by Way of Lake Chelan and Skagit River During the Months of August and September, 1882*. Washington, D.C.: U.S. Government Printing Office, 1883.

Pitzer, Paul C. *Building the Skagit*. Portland: The Galley Press, 1978.

Portman, Sally. "The Wildflowers of Sun Mountain." Pamphlet, no date.
———. *The Smiling Country*. Winthrop, Wash., 1993.
Postmarked Washington. Okanogan County Historical Society, no date.
Prentice, Rachel. "Nooksack Discovery Defies Ice-Age Theorists." *Bellingham Herald*, May 5, 1996.
Puget Sound Mail (LaConner, Wash.), October 30, 1880.
Rinehart, Mary Roberts. *My Story*. New York: Farrar & Rinehart Incorporated, 1931.
———. "Through Glacier National Park with Howard Eaton." *Collier's*, April 22, 1916, and April 29, 1916.
Roe, JoAnn. *Ghost Camps & Boom Towns*. Bellingham: Montevista Press, 1995.
———. *The North Cascadians*. Seattle: Madrona Publishers, 1980.
———. *Stevens Pass*. Seattle: The Mountaineers, 1995.
Rohn, Thomas Jesse. "Guy Waring and the Methow Trading Company, 1891–1936." University of Washington Master's Thesis.
Sampson, Chief Martin J. *Indians of Skagit County*. LaConner, Wash.: Skagit County Historical Society, 1972.
Sierra Club Bulletin, August 2, 1960.
Smith, Allan H. "Ethnography of The North Cascades." Pullman, Wash.: Center for Northwest Anthropology, Washington State University, Project Report Number 7, 1988.
Spring, Ira and Byron Fish. *Lookouts*. 1st edition. Seattle: The Mountaineers, 1981.
Steen, Harold K. "The Beginning of the National Forest System." USDA pamphlet, Forest Service FS-488, May 1991.
Thompson, Erwin N. *North Cascades N.P., Ross Lake N.R.A. & Lake Chelan N.R.A.* National Park Service, Office of History and Historic Architecture, Eastern Service Center, March 1970.
USDA Forest Service, Pacific Northwest Region, Portland, Oregon. Miscellaneous papers and references.
West, Terry L. Ph.D. "Centennial Mini-Histories of the Forest Service." USDA pamphlet, Forest Service FS-518, July 1992.
Williams, Gerald W. Ph.D. "Forest Service Organization and Reorganization: Past to Present." Paper prepared for USFS, Pacific Northwest Region, June 14, 1996.
———. "The USDA Forest Service in the Pacific Northwest: Major Political and Social Controversies between 1891–1945." Paper prepared for USFS, Pacific Northwest Region, June 30, 1994.
Willis, Margaret, ed. *Chechacos All*. Mt. Vernon, Wash., 1973.
Wilson, Bruce A. *The Late Frontier*. Okanogan, Wash., 1990.
Zim, Herbert S. and Matt N. Dodge. *The Pacific Northwest*. New York: Golden Press, 1959.

Index

Index

Acknowledgments

For granting interviews or for assistance in locating data, thanks to: Doug Albee, Franklin Barta, Howard Barta, Josephine Barta, Leona Barta Bolle, Jean Berney, Harold Bowers, Anne Braaten, Aaron Burkhart, Sr., Cindy and Genevieve Callahan, Tootsie Clark, Ken Cuthbert, Mark DeLeon, Ted Dempsey, Doug Devin, Steve Devin, Stan Dick, Elinore Drake, Barbara Duffy, Wally Eggleston, Larry Fogel and Sue Kiel of Seattle City Light, Allen G. Gibbs, Jim Harris, George Honey, Frederick W. Hubbard, Corky and Donald Hundahl, Rick Jeffreys, Dwayne Kikendall, Jean Mabry, Cal Merriman, Robert Mierendorf, Claude Miller, Steve and Mary Milka, Pat Milliren, Pat Nicholson, Bunny Olson, Jim Sandon, Wayne Stark, Jerry Sullivan, Hazel Tracy, Jon Vanderheyden, Gerald Williams, and Chuck Wolf.

Contractors in Chapter 5
Major contractors building the North Cascades Highway from 1959–72 (taken from *Pacific Builder & Engineer*, September 1, 1972):

Emil Anderson Const. Co., Ltd., Vancouver, B.C.
Butler-Jarvis, Seattle
Alfred DeCoria, Auburn
N. Fiorito Co., Seattle
Goodfellow Bros., Inc., Wenatchee
F. R. Hewett Co., Spokane
Highway Const. Co. Ltd., Vancouver, B.C.
Peter Kiewit Sons Co., Vancouver, WA
K. K. Larsen Constr. Co., Inc., Seattle
Loftus Landscaping, Inc., Kennewick
Materne Bros. Co., Spokane and Seattle
Nelson Const. Co., Ferndale
Pacific Concrete Co., Portland
Charles T. Parker Construction Co., Portland
Simpson, Gault & McKesson, Inc., Port Angeles
Snitily Bros. Const. Co., Wenatchee
Wilder Construction, Bellingham
J. E. Work, Inc., Bellevue
Paul Zimmerly Road Const., Vancouver, WA

About the Author

JoAnn Roe is the author of nine books, including *The Columbia River: A Historical Travel Guide; Stevens Pass: The Story of Railroading and Recreation in the North Cascades; Frank Matsura: Frontier Photographer,* which won the Pacific Northwest Booksellers Award for Literary Excellence and the Washington's Governor's Writers Award, and the *Marco the Manx* series of children's books. A member of the Pacific Northwest Historians Guild and the Western Writers of America, she lives in Bellingham, WA.

Other Books by JoAnn Roe:

Ghost Camps & Boom Towns (Montevista Press, 2004, ISBN 0-931551-19-6) Revision of 1995 edition, same ISBN.

Stevens Pass (Caxton Press, 2002, ISBN 0-87004-428-1) Revision and new publisher of original by The Mountaineers, 1995.

Ranald MacDonald, Pacific Rim Adventurer (WSU Press, 1997, ISBN 0-87422-146-3)

North Cascades Highway, original by The Mountaineers, 1997

Seattle Uncovered (Seaside Press, 1995, ISBN 1-55622-394-3)

Portable Writers Conference, one chapter (Quill Driver Books)

F.S. Matsura (Heibonsha, Tokyo, 1984)

The Real Old West (Douglas & McIntyre, 1981)

Frank Matsura, Frontier Photographer (Madrona Publishers, 1981)

The North Cascadians (Madrona Publishers, 1980)

Four children's books: Samurai Cat, Alaska Cat, Fisherman Cat, Castaway Cat (Montevista Press, 1984-) Published in paperback and library editions.